Autonomy and Rigid Character

Also by David Shapiro

NEUROTIC STYLES

AUTONOMY AND RIGID CHARACTER

David Shapiro

BasicBooks
A Division of HarperCollinsPublishers

Library of Congress Cataloging in Publication Data

Shapiro, David, 1926–
Autonomy and rigid character.

Includes bibliographical references and index.
1. Rigidity (Psychology) 2. Psychology, Pathological. 3. Autonomy (Psychology) 4. Obsessive-compulsive neurosis. 5. Sadism. 6. Masochism. 7. Paranoia. I. Title. [DNLM: 1. Mental disorders.
2. Neuroses. 3. Psychoses. WM 200 S532a]
RC569.5.R55S47   616.85′227   80–68953
ISBN 0-465-00567-5 (cloth)
ISBN 0-465-00568-3 (paper)

95 96 97 98 ❖/RRD H 10 9 8 7

To Julie and Benjamin

Contents

Acknowledgments

I WOULD LIKE to express my gratitude to my friend Joseph O. Chassell, M.D., of Stockbridge, Massachusetts, for his thoughtful reading of the manuscript as it was written, and for his many useful suggestions. I wish to thank also Phoebe Hoss and JoAnn Miller of Basic Books for their extremely valuable editorial help in the book's preparation. I am indebted to Margaret Thomlinson for her skillful and intelligent secretarial work. My friend Veikko A. Tähka, M.D., of Kuopio, Finland, was also helpful to me, and I should like to thank him. Finally, I wish to thank my wife, Gerry, for her judgment on innumerable matters throughout the writing.

Autonomy and Rigid Character

Introduction

IN THIS BOOK I have two principal concerns, one growing out of the other. The first issue is the general psychology of autonomy or human self-direction: the theoretical problem of autonomy as it appears in psychiatry is discussed in chapter 1; and the development of autonomy in chapter 2. The remainder of the book is devoted to the second issue, the pathology of autonomy in rigid character.

I was first led to an interest in autonomy, its subjective experience, and its pathology by an earlier interest in neurotic styles—the styles of thinking, the attitudes, and the modes of activity that characterize various neurotic conditions. It is useful, I believe, in introducing the subject of autonomy to say a few words about its relation to that earlier interest.

The relation is, in fact, quite direct and simple. It gradually became clear to me that the view of symptomatic behavior as a reflection of how individuals characteristically think and see things is in certain ways not only different from but actually contrary to the traditional dynamic view. The possibility of understanding the specific form of symptomatic behavior—for example, the constant doubting, worrying, or regretting of obsessional people—as derived from characteristic ways of thinking and points of view, reveals something fundamental about the nature of such behavior and, so to speak, the responsibility for it. It shows that there is no sharp distinction between symptomatic and nonsymptomatic volitional behavior; that even symptomatic behavior is directed not by internal forces and needs, according to their "aims,"—as traditional "dynamics" sees it—but rather by the neurotic person according to his aims, his thinking, and his point of view; and that, however strange a neurotic person's behavior may seem to us and sometimes even to him, that behavior must in some way seem to him the thing to do. The fact that neurotic people— and schizophrenic people even more so—may experience their own actions as less than autonomous, as not altogether what they wish or choose to do, but instead, for example, as the product of a "compulsion" or an irresistible impulse, does not alter this fundamental picture but only makes it more complicated and interesting. Indeed, this fact indicates the existence of a whole dimension of psychopathology, the pathology of autonomy.

The picture of human beings, including neurotic human beings, as volitional, self-directed, autonomous in this sense, is certainly not new; yet it has never been integrated into psychiatry. Psychoanalysis has historically been tied to a need-driven conception of behavior, especially symptomatic behavior, which is to say that it has seen little need at all for a theory of the processes of action, and has possessed practically no such theory, to the detriment of both its theory and its therapy. Only fairly recently has the dynamic—need-driven—conception of behavior been subject to careful theoretical criticism from the standpoint of psychoanalysis, as I shall describe shortly.

Only when one has recognized the existence of processes of autonomy or volitional direction is it possible to recognize their distortions and compromises in psychopathology. Some impairment of autonomy, I shall try to show, is intrinsic to all psychopathology. Every condition of psychopathology is characterized by modes of action that in one way or another compromise or distort normal volitional processes.

To me, the most striking distortions of these processes and also of the subjective experience of autonomy occur in the rigid self-direction of obsessive-compulsive and paranoid people. I use the term "rigid character" here in this specific sense. For reasons I shall make clear later, the distortions of the processes and the subjective experience of autonomy are central to understanding the symptomatology of these persons and the related symptomatology of sadism and masochism. Indeed, there is reason to regard these conditions of rigid character as primarily pathologies of autonomy and to assume that certain tendencies in the development of autonomy itself are central to their etiology.

In the case of obsessive-compulsive conditions, it is perhaps self-evident that a distortion of the processes of autonomy, a rigidity of self-direction, is central. I will show that the form of paranoid symptoms also, including paranoid defensiveness and projection, is a direct consequence of rigidity, but in this case, of a more severe form of it. This understanding of paranoia, I believe, helps to clarify the remarkable relationship discovered by Freud—but never, as he acknowledged, completely explained by him—between paranoid symptoms and unconscious homosexuality in men. (Why should abhorrence of homosexuality take the particular form of paranoia? Why should these individuals have such an abhorrence of homosexuality, to begin with?) In this connection, I shall re-examine the famous case of the paranoid schizophrenic Schreber, whose elaborate written account of his "nervous illness" was used by Freud in the development of his theory and remains a valuable document.

In chapters 5 and 6, I shall show how sadism and masochism, in both their sexual and nonsexual forms, can be understood as manifestations of rigid character. It is an interesting principle of the psychology of autonomy, and one that is important to the understanding of paranoid conditions and sadism and masochism as well, that the rigid person often endows relationships between superior and subordinate—relationships that figure importantly in these conditions—with special significance. I shall discuss sadism and masochism between the chapters on obsessive-compulsive and paranoid conditions because this order is helpful to understanding, and I recommend therefore that the chapters be read consecutively.

Chapter I

The Problem of Individual Autonomy

THE PROBLEM I wish to consider here is a central one in psychiatry. It is manifest in the explanation of human behavior—especially the symptomatic behavior of neurotic persons—in terms of traditional psychoanalytic "dynamics": that is, in terms of forces, drives and their derivatives, defense mechanisms, and the like. It is the problem, as I said in the introduction, of a conception of human action as given impetus and directed by internal forces according to tendencies inherent in those forces, according to their intensity and their "aims"—not as directed by the person, according to his aims, by his choice, according to his point of view and way of thinking. It is the problem, for example, of whether to conceive of an alcoholic individual as one who cannot stop drinking as much as he wants to, or as one who cannot *want* to stop drinking, much as he may think he should.

A number of psychologists—I among them—and psychoanalysts have been concerned with various aspects of this general issue in recent years. Some psychologists, essentially sympathetic to psychoanalysis, have been concerned with its basic theory of motivation, its conception of drive as force and its picture of the person as an essentially passive structure energized by the impetus of drives or their derivatives;[1] others have seen the problem as rooted in the psychoanalytic division of the personality into departments;[2] or in the absence of a picture of a personal will.[3] In my opinion, the problem requires above all an adequate conception of volition, conscious self-direction, or individual autonomy.[4]

This issue fundamentally affects our picture of a person, but it is especially acute, as I said, in connection with the understanding of neurotic individuals and symptomatic behavior. Psychiatry is full of ideas and conceptions of symptomatic behavior that, despite their wide acceptance, contain ambiguous or simply untenable assumptions regarding the nature of human action. For example, the picture of "impulse neurotics" as driven by irresistible needs or impulses or as unable to "control" their impulses; the conception of acting out; the idea of compulsive behavior, as in compulsive rituals, as driven by superego forces; the idea of repetition compulsion or the com-

---

[1]See Robert R. Holt, "Drive or Wish: A Reconsideration of the Psychoanalytic Theory of Motivation," *Psychological Issues,* vol. IX/4, Monograph 36, pp. 158–97; and George S. Klein, *Psychoanalytic Theory: An Exploration of Essentials* (New York: International Universities Press, 1976). Also, R. W. White, "Ego and Reality in Psychoanalytic Theory: A Proposal Regarding Independent Ego Energies," *Psychological Issues* (1963).

[2]Rollo May, "The Problem of Will and Intentionality in Psychoanalysis," *Contemporary Psychoanalysis* (1966) 3:55–70.

[3]Allen B. Wheelis, "Will and Psychoanalysis," *Journal of the American Psychoanalytic Association* (1956) 4:285–303; and Leslie H. Farber, *The Ways of the Will* (New York: Basic Books, 1966).

[4]For my earlier discussion of these issues, see David Shapiro, "Motivation and Action in Psychoanalytic Psychiatry," *Psychiatry* (1970) 33 (3):329–43; and David Shapiro, "Dynamic and Holistic Ideas of Neurosis and Psychotherapy," *Psychiatry* (1975) 38 (3): 218–26.

pulsion to re-enact unconscious memories; and, in fact, as far as symptomatic behavior is concerned, the general conception of unconsciously motivated behavior—all, at least on the surface, seem to suppose that particular impulses or unconscious forces provide the essential impetus and direction for—in some cases are sufficient to trigger—action. It is true that psychoanalysis has never been, in principle, unmindful of the requirements of consciousness. Motility is understood to be finally subject to consciousness, except for brief and special interruptions; impulse-driven action is regarded as being generally "ego-syntonic"; and the symptomatic behavior of neurosis is understood to require, as it were, at least the clothing of conscious purpose, achieved through rationalization, symbolic substitution, and so on. Nevertheless, the role assigned by the dynamic view to consciousness in symptomatic behavior is essentially compliant and innocuous—for that reason, such behavior is usually described in psychiatry as "irrational" or inappropriate—and such a role does not provide a true picture of adult action.

In adult human beings, even strong impulses account only for strong temptations; they do not in themselves account for actions. Action involves more complicated processes. Human beings are endowed with imagination, and imaginative consciousness, and thus cannot act, even if they want to, without a certain degree of conscious anticipation and intention. A particular feeling or urge will not trigger action of any extensiveness but will only generate awareness of the possibilities of action and give rise to some form of conscious intention. Thus, action will involve the attitudes of consciousness, characteristic points of view, ways of thinking, which shape the subjective world. These shape the experience of motivation and the significance of any anticipated action and in that sense are the final determinants of action. If action is viewed as the product not merely of impulses but also of ways of thinking, points of view, attitudes of consciousness, even symptomatic behavior, as I shall try to show, no longer seems irrational or inappropriate. Such behavior becomes understandable in terms not only of the past but also of present subjective necessities. Indeed, such behavior becomes understandable from this standpoint even when the subject himself, only dimly aware of his own attitudes and point of view, does not recognize it as the product of his own wish and intention.

This view sees behavior not as driven by impulse according to its "aims" but as directed by a person according to his aims: it is self-directed, even when, as in the case of symptomatic behavior, it may not be fully experienced as such. This distinction reveals the essential deficiency of traditional dynamic understanding as far as psychotherapy is concerned. Insofar as dynamic understanding slights the attitudes and processes of consciousness that finally determine action, it obscures the fact and the nature of the person's authorship of his own actions —when it is the essential aim of psychotherapy to introduce him to his authorship and to enlarge his experience of it.[5] (The same deficiency is responsible for the dynamic theory's failure to achieve a satisfactory understanding of the specific forms of neurotic symptoms, the problem, so-called, of the "choice of neurosis." It is possible to understand the disposition to specific symptoms only through an appreciation of the individual's contemporary attitudes and ways of thinking.)

The dynamic conception was a product of Freud's search for processes in mental life that could account for symptomatic

---

[5]For a clear discussion of this aim of psychotherapy, see Hellmuth Kaiser, "The Problem of Responsibility in Psychotherapy," *Psychiatry* (1955) 18: 205–11; also in L. B. Fierman (ed.), *Effective Psychotherapy: The Contribution of Hellmuth Kaiser* (New York: Free Press, 1965). This problem of psychoanalytic therapy is also addressed by Roy Schafer, *Language and Insight* (New Haven: Yale University Press, 1978).

behavior, precisely that kind of behavior for which consciously articulated, "rational" intentions or "will" could not account. In a sense the conception was the product of his respect for the least and most specific irrational details of these symptoms and of his insistence on their significance. He discovered their causes in previously unrecognized unconscious processes—first repressed affects, later drives and the conflicts around them which manifested themselves in various derivative and disguised forms in symptoms. Freud's program was thus one of discovery of hidden sources of behavior, first in their disguised manifestations in symptoms, then—confirming their existence as general human tendencies—in various areas of normal life. It was an enormously successful program. But its very success in identifying such hidden processes, particularly as manifested in highly specific or short-lived specimens of behavior, led to a certain neglect and underestimation of other aspects of the person and worked a distortion in the conception of behavior in general. In the analysis of the sources of behavior there was no theory of action.

There is still no adequate theory of action—and in particular, of symptomatic or unconsciously motivated action. Psychoanalysis is certainly no simple theory of drive-activated behavior; it has developed, especially in the years since Freud, elaborate conceptions of the regulation and adaptation—the "taming"—of drives.[6] But these conceptions are not sufficient to meet the problem of volitional action as long as the impetus of action is conceived to be drive or need, tamed or not—especially unconscious drive or need.[7] Indeed, these theoretical

[6]See David Rapaport, "The Conceptual Model of Psychoanalysis" (pp. 405–31) and David Rapaport, "Some Metapsychological Considerations Concerning Activity and Passivity" (pp. 530–68), both in *The Collected Papers of David Rapaport*, Merton M. Gill, ed. (New York: Basic Books, 1967).

[7]For a more detailed discussion of the relation of psychoanalytic concepts of drive regulation to volitional action, see Shapiro, "Motivation and Action in Psychoanalytic

conceptions have hardly affected the dynamic picture of symptomatic action at all.

There is no doubt that the psychology of action—that is, of volition—has also been dogged by certain logical or philosophical problems. I am referring to the vitalistic conception of a will that transcends psychological cause, explanation, and predictability, and to the old philosophical problem of free will versus determinism—the problem of reconciling volitional experience with the assumption of a lawful, understandable, and predictable universe. Psychologists have assumed (reasonably in my opinion)—and Freud must have as well—that the phenomena of subjective experience must ultimately be explained by non-subjective (or, at least, not merely subjective) processes. And this assumption, in turn, has been commonly thought to require that the subjective experience of volition must be explained merely as the subjective effect of some form of prior nonsubjective impetus such as drive. Either such explanation —or slip into vitalism and a vitalistic notion of free will. But this assumption, like the problem of free will or determinism, confronts us with spurious alternatives. It identifies the requirements of scientific explanation with what is actually only a particular kind of scientific explanation. It is a kind of scientific explanation that, in fact, cannot explain the subjective sensation of volition or free choice, because it does not recognize the actual volitional processes that underlie it.[8]

Psychiatry" [4]. In brief, the conception of the progressive modulation and adaptive "taming"—by structures of the ego—of drives and needs is aimed at explaining the development from a condition of helpless, immediate motor discharge to one of realistic, effective, purposive (goal-seeking) action. Tamed, reality-adapted needs, the impetus of action, are coordinated through cognitive processes with routes or means of action through which they may be satisfied. Thus the conception is consistent with the dynamic viewpoint. See footnote 8 below.

[8]Robert P. Knight tackled the problem of volitional experience from the standpoint of the dynamic and structural ideas of psychoanalysis and probably got as far as that

The dynamic or impetus-driven understanding of behavior cannot, in my opinion, account for volitional experience, or encompass volitional action, essentially because it underestimates the motivational significance of human imaginativeness. It recognizes imaginativeness and anticipation only in their instrumental function, their function of finding routes of satisfaction for prior need or impetus; whereas, in fact, imagination and anticipation determine the final form and even the existence of effective impetus. This last point is also made by those psychoanalytic psychologists who have proposed substituting the concept of wish for that of drive.[9] A wish is a motivation that may include anticipation of action and is formed out of an intrinsically imaginative relationship of the person to the external world. It seems necessary, however, to go further than the substitution of the one concept for the other. If human motivation implies imagination and anticipation of action, its form will depend on the nature of one's cognitive relationship with the world and it will certainly be necessary to speak of various forms of motivation: one could not reasonably, for example, describe as a wish the hunger of a newborn infant. Furthermore, wish alone does not seem sufficient to explain the nature or the experience of volitional action. (In particular, the concept of unconscious wish—insofar as its relationship to conscious intention and action remains ambiguous—seems to leave the problem of symptomatic behavior about where it was.) For this, we need an enlarged picture of the imaginative

standpoint will allow: he attempted to explain the subjective experience of free choice in terms of the ego's smooth and effective regulation of motivational impetus, but he was finally obliged to argue that the experience is only one of being in harmony with internal necessity ("Determinism, 'Freedom' and Psychotherapy," in R. P. Knight and C. R. Friedman [eds.], *Psychoanalytic Psychiatry and Psychology, Clinical and Theoretical Papers, Austen Riggs Center, vol I.* [New York: International Universities Press, 1954]).

[9]Holt, "Drive or Wish" [1], Klein, *Psychoanalytic Theory* [1]. Also George S. Klein, *Perception, Motives, and Personality* (New York: Alfred A. Knopf, 1970).

processes of such action, a picture in which those processes will be the context of the sensation of wish, of need, perhaps even of drive. This will be a picture, in short, not only of the nature of motivations but, specifically, of the processes involved in how a person acts.[10]

Terms like "will" and "volition" are ambiguous in their connotations; it is better to talk for the time being simply of the self-directedness of behavior. We have no reason to find human self-directedness intrinsically puzzling or philosophically doubtful. We recognize self-regulation of various sorts not only in other living organisms and in biological processes but also in certain kinds of machines, organizations, and even political entities. The functions of the organism, for example —or the activity of the organism as a whole—are regulated by processes internal to it. These processes confer a certain degree of autonomy, of independence of circumstance and surroundings, and endow the organism with a range of adaptability. In none of these cases do we regard self-regulation or autonomy as tainted with vitalism, or requiring any notion of free will, or implying any exception to natural law or predictability.[11] The more autonomous and independent of its immediate surroundings and circumstances an organism is, however, and the

---

[10]Schafer (*Language and Insight* [5]) proposes an "action language" to replace the language of dynamics (forces, drives, defense mechanisms, and so forth) in psychological description and in psychotherapy. By denoting as actions behavioral, motivational, and other psychological processes, he attempts to recognize the person—rather than, for example, the drive or the superego—as the author or "agent" of action. Schafer, it seems to me, carries a good idea too far. It is obviously valuable both theoretically and therapeutically to recognize intention and action in symptomatic behavior or in certain psychological processes where they might not have been recognized before (cf. Kaiser, "Problem of Responsibility" [5] and my remarks about Kaiser in notes 16, 17, 19, this chapter); but indiscriminately to describe as actions psychological processes and conditions, such as emotions and beliefs, is simply unconvincing and seems doctrinaire. Such a program tends to confuse the meaning of action.

[11]The general point of view here is in agreement with the model of a self-governing organism outlined by Robert R. Holt in "On Freedom, Autonomy and the Redirection of Psychoanalytic Theory: A Rejoinder," *International Journal of Psychiatry* (1967) 3:524–36.

greater its range of adaptability, the more difficult it is likely to be to predict its behavior.

Perhaps a distinction can be made, although it cannot be a sharp one, between self-regulation and its particular and advanced form which might be called "self-direction." For example, the instinctive activities of animals constitute a certain kind of self-regulation and confer a certain level of autonomy. A thirsty animal instinctively seeks and responds to water; a deficiency or an imbalance of the organism vis-à-vis its environment is corrected by a complicated process of activity, triggered by the imbalance or the availability of what is needed and executed by the animal itself. The limitations of such autonomy, however, and the limited sense in which one can speak of such behavior as self-directed—if one can do so at all—become obvious in comparison with the human being's capacity to anticipate and plan for his own maintenance and the satisfaction of his needs. An animal's instinctive self-maintaining activity is determined by inherent biological tendencies. Yet one cannot comfortably say that it is directed by the animal; one might rather say the reverse—as in fact one does when one speaks of an animal as being driven by thirst.

The early instinctive behavior of human infants is in some respects comparable; elementary needs or discomforts trigger certain kinds of activity—crying, searching for the breast, sucking movements—which signal to the environment that the infant needs care. It is no doubt true in the case of such infant behavior, as it often is in nature, that what may appear to be purposive or intentional is actually not, but is merely reflexive or instinctive reaction to certain sensations.

As the human being develops, however, the range and the variety of behavior are enormously increased, and a new level of autonomy is achieved. Self-awareness and a consciousness of —a capacity to imagine—the possibilities of action on the external world develop with enormous consequences for the child's relationship with the world. That relationship rapidly becomes very much more active. Behavior that is merely reactive is increasingly replaced by intentional action. Less and less is behavior immediately triggered by particular needs and less and less is its direction determined by instinctive tendencies or by the tendencies inherent in those needs. Behavior comes to be determined by far more complex processes which are integrative and imaginative and supersede the demands of particular momentary needs or of immediate surroundings. A new kind of self-regulation comes into being in the form of increasingly articulated conscious aims, and with it a new kind of behavior, intentional, planful action—self-directed action in the proper sense.

The distinction between instinctive behavior and action that follows from conscious aim might be compared with the difference between social movement in a crowd or society without plan or conscious organization and planned social change. In a society without plan, changes and movements occur, but the whole society changes as a more or less direct consequence of the activity of particular groups or individuals in pursuit of their own aims. The society as a whole cannot properly be said to possess aims or to be self-directing, though it certainly may have directional tendencies and even the appearance of purposefulness. In a planned, organized society, such particular pressures are superseded by another, perhaps integrative, agency that is not totally dependent on nor immediately responsive to any of them and can plan for the society as a whole. (This historical development is the Marxist dream. Marx saw the advent of socialism not merely as another, more advanced, stage of society but also as marking a new level of human autonomy, social autonomy, in which society would no longer be driven by blind economic tendencies but would be purposefully directed according to human values. Society would then advance, in the Marxist phrase, from the "realm of necessity to the realm of freedom.")

In the human adult almost no extensive action is a simple immediate reaction to a particular need or opportunity; virtually all action is to some extent self-directed and planned. It is not possible, even if one desired to do so, to act immediately, without anticipation, imagination, and some degree of consciousness of the self acting—except perhaps in the case of the most severe pathology. Needs, interests, wishes, the opportunities of circumstance—instead of triggering reactions as in infancy—generate interest in the possibilities of action. In the most articulated case, the imagination of possibilities of action culminates in a conclusive wish to act, in a choice or a decision, in an intention. This process—which occurs rapidly, continually, and largely unnoticed—is the essential process that leads to action; its product, the impetus to action, comes into existence only when the process culminates in an intention. The intention is the impetus to act. This is not the impetus of needs or drives toward an object; it is the impetus to action of a person conscious of the possibilities of action, a person who sees these possibilities, therefore, according to his own attitudes and ways of thinking and also his other interests. This is why the quality—such as impetuous or deliberate—of an action will be as characteristic of the person as it will reflect the intensity of a particular need or wish.

This kind of action is what we call "volitional action;" and this kind of conscious intention, in its more deliberate forms and especially when it is sufficiently strong to override obstacles or more immediate temptations, is what we call "will." The capacity for such action is the basis not merely of a comparative independence from the immediate environment but of an active mastery of the environment. It is also the basis for the human sense of autonomy. The experience of the imaginative process, the trying on of possibilities, which culminates in an impetus to act, in an intention, is the experience of choosing, of freedom of action, of being one's own master.

To say that human action is always to some degree volitional and guided by conscious aims is not to say that all action is entirely deliberate or that every piece of behavior is planned and consciously purposeful. Nor does it mean that the aims of action are necessarily completely consciously articulated or self-conscious. Intentionality and the capacity for volitional action develop gradually and through a number of phases in childhood and, in adulthood, have a great range and variety of forms. Individuals have different and characteristic tendencies in articulation of aim, in level of intentionality, and in style of action and corresponding differences in volitional experience.

Two neurotic modes of volitional action—that of hysterical and impulsive characters and certain passive "weak" individuals, and that of rigid characters—serve to illustrate the variety of forms of conscious self-direction. Among the former, aims and purposes are often exceedingly vague, and intentions are hardly articulated or self-conscious. Such a person may *feel* that he has virtually no aims of his own, that his actions are entirely determined by force of circumstance, by the expectations of others, that they are a reflexive—or even irresistible—response to opportunity. Such a person may say, "I didn't mean to, I just did it," or "I didn't want to, but he asked me to." Such disavowals of conscious intention are impossible to credit completely, but there is no doubt that consciousness of intention, deliberateness, and planfulness have all been diminished; at the same time there is a tendency to quick and relatively spur-of-the-moment action.[12] Among rigid characters, on the other hand, there is an extraordinary degree of articulation and self-consciousness of aim and purpose, an often excruciating consciousness of choice and decision, and great deliberateness of action.

It seems clear also that volitional direction of behavior operates in a hierarchical way: that is, it permits various degrees of spontaneity or immediacy of reaction. For example, many kinds of habitual or quasi-automatic behavior—such as driving, typing, or speaking—are initiated and in a general way guided by conscious aims even though their technical operation follows automatized patterns. In such behavior (which probably includes aspects of all behavior) habitual or automatized reaction is consciously permitted within certain limits. The fact that a certain permissive consciousness of general aims is not altogether absent from such behavior becomes evident when its permissible limits are approached; consciousness of action then becomes greater, and action becomes more deliberate. One may seem to be driving automatically, while talking or thinking of other things, but when the destination approaches or when road conditions change, one drives more carefully and deliberately. The situation is much the same for spontaneity of behavior, for relatively immediate and unpremeditated, spur-of-the-moment reaction. The witty person reserves his wit for certain occasions; even the bad-tempered man calms down when a neighbor appears on the scene and, however angry he may be, he is much less likely to fly off the handle at work than at home. In general, for appreciable periods of time, volitional direction and control of behavior may be largely unnoticed and may consist essentially of a benign peripheral awareness of one's activity, within certain limits determined by general pur-

[12]For a discussion of the attitudes and modes of action of hysterical and impulsive characters, see my *Neurotic Styles* (New York: Basic Books, 1965).

pose or attitude.

Probably most of our behavior is of this sort, relatively spontaneous, often without articulated purpose, but ultimately guided by interests and attitudes that become articulated and self-conscious only from time to time, and then perhaps incompletely. There are, of course, striking and characteristic individual differences in the style of this kind of hierarchical self-direction and in the degree and the kind of permissible spontaneity.

Neurosis and the Problem of Unconsciously Motivated Action

The most difficult problem to be accounted for by a theory of consciously directed, volitional, action is that of unconscious motivation as it appears in neurosis. Perhaps it is the most difficult problem for a "holistic" psychology or for any conception of a more or less unified "self." It is not the existence of unconscious feelings or motivations themselves that poses the problem; it is not difficult, for example, to assume that unconscious feelings or motivations may contribute to or affect the conscious aims of volitional action. But the matter, insofar as it involves neurosis, is more complicated. Neurosis confronts us with a picture of conflict and schism in the personality which is not necessarily represented in consciously articulated motivations and intentions; with behavior that may be at odds with these articulated motivations and intentions and cannot possibly be explained by them; with symptomatic behavior for which no motivation at all may be consciously recognized, and which may even be contrary to consciously articulated interests and attitudes. The evidence of such symptomatic behavior does indeed seem to support a picture of behavior directly driven by the impetus of unconscious needs or impulses.

Just such explanations of unconsciously motivated behavior are in fact commonplace in psychiatry. A gambler who loses, a criminal who is caught, are said to have unconsciously sought and accomplished those ends.

A successful business executive, accused of forging checks for large sums, explains his past behavior according to what he has learned from his recent psychotherapy: "Clearly, there were forces at work within me that I was not consciously aware of," and he adds that his professional success "required me to start punishing myself."[13]

Such explanations of action are, at best, vague and incomplete and, more likely, not tenable explanations of human action at all; for they imply that an unconscious motive may be responsible for action by a fully conscious person virtually without regard to his conscious disposition, his attitudes—all that comes into play in human action. The tradition that accepts unconscious needs or wishes as sufficient explanation for action without reference to conscious attitudes and disposition may credit even the most far-fetched explanations of behavior. Even if we accept the existence of such needs or wishes as those I cited, they could not by themselves adequately explain such action. Even among successful businessmen who may, consciously or unconsciously, feel guilty, after all, few forge checks.

In this context it may be more than a truism to observe that

[13]Reported in *Los Angeles Times*, 12 July 1979.

no action is out of character. And this is so precisely because action, especially extensive action, involves more than an impetus of need. Action is "in character" because it is, finally, a product of imaginative processes, attitudes of consciousness, frames of mind that give it the stamp of character. This is why even the strangest symptomatic behavior of the neurotic person turns out to reflect attitudes, ways of thinking, frames of mind characteristic of that person.[14] The neurotic person who carries out compulsive rituals—rituals that seem strange and alien even to him—will also be characterized in other areas by a rigid, perhaps dutiful, observance of authoritative rules and principles of behavior. It is, in fact, only through understanding the characteristic attitudes, ways of thinking and points of view that shape consciousness that it is possible to understand the subjective necessity for such strange behavior. Only through such an understanding, again, can symptomatic behavior be seen not merely as the product of an irrational intrusion from the past or from the unconscious, but as the product of a contemporary state of mind.

This is just the problem. On the one hand, the symptomatic behavior of the neurotic person is "in character": it reflects the attitudes and the ways of thinking that generally characterize his consciousness and guide his action. On the other hand, he does not seem to completely recognize himself in this behavior; he may experience his own behavior as strange or peculiar, as something he does not entirely want or even intend to do— for example, as the result of a "compulsion" or an "irresistible impulse." Thus, we are confronted with behavior that in some sense is certainly consciously directed, yet in some sense seems not to be.

[14]See Shapiro, *Neurotic Styles* [12].

For example, a young woman, a former beauty queen, referring to her date the previous evening, says ruefully to her therapist, "Well, I did my number again last night. That's three times with three different men in one week. I tell them, 'Gee, I never met anyone like you before.' " Each time her behavior has the same effect: the man, flattered, becomes an eager suitor. But she has no further interest in them, does not even wish to see them again. Why, then, she asks, does she do this? She does not intend to, she says. She sees no gain in it, she doesn't like it in herself, she knows it is "manipulative," but to what purpose? The only result that she can see is that the men become pests.

But as she talks further, it becomes apparent that her "number" is not limited to a few apparently impulsive, "unintended" remarks. She sets the stage for such encounters, plans the evening, dresses carefully. In fact, she then remembers with a laugh that whenever she meets a man, she sizes him up and takes note of whether he will be an "easy" or, more rarely, "a difficult case"; and these men, of course, she is more interested in.

It is not possible to believe that this woman's "number," as she describes her behavior, does not in some sense reflect conscious intention; indeed, she confirms the existence of such intention, actually remembers its conscious existence (and not only in the cases at hand but also in others). Yet it is equally clear that her behavior was not consciously directed in a complete sense. It was guided by a conscious aim, but it was not completely self-conscious. Its aim was conscious, yet not consciously articulated.

In order to understand this phenomenon more clearly, it is necessary to consider certain aspects of the nature of neurosis or neurotic character. Neurosis in one way or another restricts subjective experience. Neurotic attitudes and ways of thinking, having developed in shrinking or self-protective reaction to certain kinds of conflict or discomfort, then tend to inhibit the full conscious experience of certain sorts of conflictful and discomforting feelings or motivations. It is not merely the conscious experience of particular memories, feelings, or wishes that is inhibited, but whole classes of subjective experience inimical to these attitudes are also inhibited. Thus, the guarded and defensive attitudes of some persons of rigid character tend to inhibit the full conscious development of certain kinds of emotional experience. In such a person, for example, an incipient feeling of admiration or affection for another person may immediately give rise to, and be experienced as, a sensation of weakness or softness; and this sensation will in turn trigger a reactive intensification of guardedness and a contraction of the original emotion. In this respect neurotic attitudes and ways of thinking perform the functions that psychoanalysis has traditionally attributed to the various defense mechanisms. The discomforting experience of certain feelings and motivations that are inimical to the neurotic person's attitudes triggers compensating reactions according to those attitudes that diminish or inhibit the discomforting experience. The function of defense in neurosis simply describes the ways in which neurotic character, once formed, tends to retain stability.

This process, however, is not necessarily complete. Perhaps it can never be complete. It can diminish or inhibit the full conscious development of a feeling or an interest, perhaps even eliminate any further awareness of it, but the process is not likely to eliminate the interest or feeling altogether. Let me give an example to make this more clear.

The compulsive person with worried and careful attitudes may experience as reckless or irresponsible an unusual enthusiasm or a temptation to do something—say, take a trip—which deviates from his usual dutiful routine. This anxiety prompts an intensification of worry and precautionary search for possibilities of risks or problems, a search that cannot be concluded until he finds some risks or problems with at least a semblance of plausibility. At this point, the discomforting temptation, or at least his awareness of any enthusiasm for it, is diminished. Yet it is entirely possible that he will still take the trip, only he will take it worriedly.

Such a person may say, "I'm doing it [taking the trip, buying the car, perhaps even getting married], but I don't really want to," "It's sure to be a failure," "I know it's a mistake," or the like.

Listening to such gloomy forebodings, which are so conspicuously contradicted by behavior, one has the impression that the speaker himself does not actually believe, certainly does not fully believe, what he is saying, and that if he did, he would surely act differently. Yet there is little doubt that he thinks he believes what he is saying. In other words, an estrangement has developed between how this person thinks he feels, on the one hand, and how he actually feels and behaves, on the other. This is not estrangement between conscious and unconscious feelings. It is a gap—or, perhaps more precisely, an incomplete congruence—between what he self-consciously recognizes, identifies, or articulates as his feelings and the actual, though unrecognized and unarticulated, nature of his subjective experience—the actual quality of his wishes, the actual direction of his interest and attention, his actual frame of mind, estimate of his prospects, all that actually accounts for his actions.[15]

[15] I have considered whether this kind of subjective experience might be described with the psychoanalytic term "preconscious," but I do not think it would be accurate. That term, in any case, is not sufficiently descriptive.

In neurotic persons such estrangements exist in more or less stable forms. The neurotic process has created an articulation of consciousness that does not represent but in fact distorts actual feelings, wishes, interests, intentions, the actual state of subjective experience. Thus, neurotic people often think that they want or are interested in what actually they only believe they should want or be interested in; they imagine that they are, and often act, angrier or less angry than they feel; they believe that they intend to do what they have no intention of doing; they think that they feel kind or sympathetic to someone else when their interest is not so much in that person as in themselves, in being kind or sympathetic; they think that they feel humble when in fact they are proud of their humility; they believe that they feel confident, they try to act confident, when their actual subjective experience, the expression in their voice and in their eyes, is anything but confident.

> Thus a young man, speaking of a recent decision to take a certain job, says emphatically, "I'm sure it's the right thing to do! . . . I guess."

Sometimes the estrangement of articulated feelings and intentions from what the neurotic person actually feels or intends is reflected in a conspicuous discrepancy between those articulated feelings and actual behavior (as in the case of the man who says, and thinks, "I don't really want to do it," and does it). Often, however, this estrangement is reflected only in a certain quality of distortion or ungenuineness in what the neurotic person says or does or, rather, in how he says or does it. The behavior of these persons often seems forced or exaggerated, artificial in some way. This is manifest in the case of the man I just cited when he says with an exaggerated confidence, "I'm sure it's the right thing to do!" Hellmuth Kaiser was, to my knowledge, the first to focus attention on this phenomenon; he said that the neurotic person is not completely "behind" what he says or does.[16]

For example, a young man expresses concern over the health of an older man, but his behavior seems forced, overly solicitous, perhaps even patronizing.

A woman behaves with a humility and deference so exaggerated that it makes the person who is its object uncomfortable and even uncertain whether she is being serious or ironic.

A young man says with a concern that seems somewhat artificial, "I must control my temper!" referring to the previous night's scene with his wife. But as he continues to describe, somewhat theatrically, his intimidating and "uncontrollable" outbursts and his wife's cowering, a smile begins to play around the corners of his mouth. When the smile is called to his attention, he irritably brushes the subject of his expression aside as trivial and tries to look sober.

Such behavior is artificial certainly; it misrepresents—even to himself—the subject's feelings and intentions. Yet this behavior, however artificial, must be a product of genuine feelings and intentions of some kind. The solicitous man imagines himself to be motivated by feelings of kindness and respectful concern, but in fact his concern is to behave in the right way, to have the proper feelings. It is to that matter that his attention and his effort are primarily directed, and flickering sensations of contrary feelings prompt him to double his efforts. But

[16]Kaiser, "Problem of Responsibility" [5].

he does not, cannot, notice this process; he is wrapped up in achieving its result. The deferential woman sees herself as humble and would describe herself so, but in fact her subjective experience is not of humility. She is pridefully, resentfully, conscious of her lesser position, and she declares it and its moral superiority to herself as well as to the other: this is her "humility." The man who thinks himself concerned about his "temper" is actually pleased with his manliness and his power to intimidate his wife. His unwilling smile reflects this subjective experience, his satisfaction in having exercised his power to some effect. This pleasure is conscious, but he does not notice it and is not conscious of experiencing it.

The symptomatic behavior of these neurotic persons is not directed or triggered by the impetus of unconscious impulse or wish; it is the product of an unrecognized frame of mind, of attitudes, feelings, and intentions that are present in or characterize conscious experience. There is no doubt, however, that these unrecognized and unarticulated feelings and intentions are conscious only in a limited sense; nor that the action that is their product is self-directed only in a limited sense. To the extent that interests and intentions lack articulation and self-consciousness—these are certainly matters of degree—the imaginative, flexible, planful entertainment of possibilities of action is diminished. This describes, in fact, the behavior of neurotic persons: it tends to be either rigid or impulsive, to be either directed according to fixed, a priori rules or principles, themselves lacking in conscious articulation, or comparatively unreflective, planless, spur of the moment.

The impairment of the processes of self-direction or autonomy manifest in action of this kind is also reflected, as some of my examples have already suggested, in corresponding kinds of impairment of the subjective experience of freedom of action, of choice, or of having intended and chosen to do what one has done.[17] (Kaiser describes this impairment as a loss of the feeling of "responsibility" for one's action.)[18]

The neurotic person may liken himself to a train running efficiently along set tracks, on the one hand, or to a leaf floating with the current, on the other. He may say, "I'm going to do it, but I don't really want to," "I don't want to, but I must," "I want to, but I can't," "I didn't want to, but I couldn't help it," and so on.

The fact that neurosis involves a loss of autonomy of this kind helps to explain certain of the effects of psychotherapy. The therapist's articulation of the patient's previously unrecognized motivation or intention in connection, say, with a recent action may have two effects that might easily seem paradoxical. On the one hand, while the patient may previously have regarded his behavior merely as puzzling, unwished, a compulsion, a lapse of will, or a weakness of character (for example, "I really want to stop drinking, but I'm not strong enough"), he now experiences it as having been his choice and his intention. He recognizes that in the circumstances he wanted to do what he did—if not for gain, then to prevent loss; if not for pleasure, then for necessary relief. He realizes that his action seemed to him at the time the only thing to do, and that he could not have wanted to do otherwise, though someone else might have. He may well realize that he has every intention of doing so again.

---

[17]In the case of schizophrenia, it appears that the actual impairment of volitional processes, with the result of rigid and stereotyped behavior or impulsiveness, and the corresponding impairment and distortion of the subjective experience of autonomy, may both be more marked. Cf. Kurt Goldstein, "Methodological Approach to the Study of Schizophrenic Thought Disorder," in J. S. Kasanin (ed.), *Language and Thought in Schizophrenia* (New York: W. W. Norton, 1964).

[18]Kaiser, "Problem of Responsibility" [5].

At the same time and for the same reason, this enlargement of his subjective experience, or enlarged consciousness of it, brings with it a greater sense of freedom of choice, and a greater actuality of choice, in the matter. To be conscious of his intention and his aim is to experience himself as the author of his action in both the past and the future; or—to put it another way—it is to create a more active relationship between him and that objective aim. If he is to act in the same way again he must now *plan* to do so. Thus, both an actual increase of autonomy and an increased sense of autonomy are automatically effected in an individual by the conscious articulation of his intention and aim. Such an articulation makes inevitable what was previously not possible: the objective imagination of alternatives and consequently the greater reality of choice.[19]

The Significance of Autonomy for Rigid Character

A few words should be said here concerning the remainder of this book and the relation of autonomy, as I have discussed it so far, to the subject of rigid character. The psychology of individual autonomy or self-direction has two kinds of psychiatric significance. It has, first, the general significance I have discussed: it suggests a general view of action and of symptomatic behavior and also certain general conclusions concerning psychopathology. Insofar as all psychopathology involves internal conflict and some estrangement from motivation and in-

[19]Kaiser ("Problem of Responsibility" [5]) regards this therapeutic effect, at least in its subjective aspect of the patient's increased sense of responsibility for his action, as the central therapeutic effect. Schafer (*Language and Insight* [5]) also emphasizes the same therapeutic effect which he describes as the patient's experience of himself as the agent of his behavior—and to Schafer, also, apparently, of his feelings.

tention, it will involve some loss of autonomy as well—probably, the more severe the pathology, the greater the loss. In addition to its general significance for psychopathology, autonomy or self-direction has its own development, in the course of which it may itself be a subject of conflict and thus liable to certain developmental distortions. In other words, not only is an impairment of autonomy a symptom, a manifestation, of all psychopathology, but developmental conflicts around, and subsequent distortions of, autonomy can be a central and independent source of psychopathology. Such appears to be true of the various forms of rigid character whose study occupies most of this book.

In these cases a form of self-direction and volitional action has developed—a form of "will" if one likes—which retains many of the features of the child's relationship to the superior authority of the adult and the authoritative rules laid down by adults. It is a will that is intrinsically ambivalent and intrinsically rigid. In these persons the rigidity of self-direction itself —or, more exactly, the attitudes and the modes of thinking that such rigidity is comprised of—seem to be the essential agency of the neurotic self-estrangement. In this specific sense these conditions of rigid character seem to be pathologies of autonomy.

Chapter 2

The Development of Autonomy

IN THIS CHAPTER, I review—with the help of some data from developmental psychology, particularly Piaget's—certain aspects of the development of self-direction and individual autonomy. I have several purposes in doing so. I wish to show something of the nature of early intentionality, of what could perhaps be called "prevolitional self-direction," in order to give some insight into the processes of purposeful and intentional action whose aims are not yet consciously articulated. I wish also to show the important relationship between the development of autonomy and the development of an objective attitude toward the external world. This relationship seems to me central to the understanding of autonomy. I believe that it will also help to clarify the severe loss of reality in paranoid conditions. My main purpose, however, is simply to examine closely the meaning of autonomy, with a view both to its general psychiatric significance and its special significance for rigid character, through its various developmental forms from infantile intentionality through the capacity for genuine volitional action and will to the adolescent's assertion of personal authority.

It has been said that the child's increasing independence of the immediate impact of his present environment is a general trend of human development.[1] In psychoanalytic psychology, the processes of "internalization"—that is, the processes of internal representation of external reality—are regarded as central to this aspect of development. These are of two kinds. One kind of internalization is represented, for example, in the achievement of automatic internal signals associated with danger that enable the child to avoid certain dangers; internal regulations also inhibit certain behavior that might be prohibited and punishable. In general, however, the development of internal signals and regulations is far less significant for the child's independence from his immediate environment than the development of imagination and thought, which internalize external reality in a different sense. Imagination and thought provide an awareness of a world wider than the one that is immediately present. They, therefore, not only dilute the impact of the present but also open avenues for action beyond the present.

Let me put the matter in a biological context. A child in relation to his environment is initially more helpless than any other immature animal, and he remains helpless for a long time. Humans are not well provided with the specifically adaptive instinctive patterns of response that appear in lower animals soon after birth. The animal that cannot swim is likely to have an instinctive aversion to water, but the child who cannot swim may well find the water attractive. The animal never loses

[1] Heinz Hartmann, *Essays on Ego Psychology* (New York: International Universities Press, 1965), p. 41.

its dependence on the present environment. It never loses its immediate, reflexive, or instinctive reactions to the cues of its environment or its dependence on these cues. Its survival depends on these reactions. On the other hand, the human's lack of tight coordination through instinctive response patterns to a specific environment is an essential condition for the enormously greater flexibility of human adaptation. It is not only that the human's reactions to the environment, being originally more diffuse and unspecific, are more plastic and educable, but also, as I have said, that his behavior, during a long and complicated development, comes to be determined primarily by processes other than his reaction to the present environment. The development of thought and imagination and of an objective attitude toward the external world liberates him from the impact of his present environment and fundamentally changes his whole relationship to it. He is liberated from a passive and immediate reactiveness to the present environment by the appearance of increasingly articulated aims which extend beyond the present environment. The pursuit of these conscious aims—deliberate, planned, conscious action—supersedes mere reactiveness. This is the key to human flexibility.

This development is a more extended process than might be imagined. Consider how much of everyone's picture of the childlike reflects in various ways the child's limited self-direction. I am speaking, for example, of the normal child's spontaneity, immediacy of reaction and, in a sense, irresponsibility, his distractability and openness to impression, his lack of self-consciousness. It is normally not until the end of adolescence that such planning, including planning for life, and the sense of personal weight that gives it seriousness, is fully developed; and it is, I believe, the achievement of that psychological autonomy that marks the end of adolescence in the most definite way.

There are, of course, factors other than those I have in-dicated involved in the development of autonomy; the most obvious are physical growth and muscular development, motility and competency. There are landmarks of physical development, such as the development of bowel control, that are also landmarks of the development of autonomy. But the development of autonomy or self-direction cannot be iden-tified with a particular brief phase of child development such as that which corresponds to the development of bowel control.

There is no doubt that bowel control constitutes a significant advance in volitional control and in the child's mastery of himself. A kind of autonomy is achieved at that time—an "experience of the autonomy of free choice,"[2] as Erikson puts it—and is manifest in the child's willfulness and significant for the future development of his personality. It would be too narrow and restrictive a definition, however, to identify the achievements of this developmental phase with the overall achievement of autonomy or self-direction; for in this general sense, the achievement of individual autonomy is not a phase of child development but extends throughout that develop-ment and itself has numerous phases. (This view seems in principle consistent with Erikson's. In his well-known chart of the eight stages of development,[3] Erikson makes clear that precursors of the volitional capacity, tendencies present "from the beginning," must be allowed for, and that he regards each stage not merely as a prototype but as a basis for further development.)

The general development of autonomy, as I shall try to show in this chapter, reflects the development of the mind—of "in-telligence" in Piaget's general sense—and the changing rela-

[2]Erik H. Erikson, *Childhood and Society* (New York: W. W. Norton, 1950), p. 222.
[3]Ibid., p. 234.

tions between the individual and the external world which are a part of that development. That development, above all, accounts for human self-direction and its various stages and forms.

There is no fully volitional action or genuine self-direction without a capacity for abstract thought. This capacity implies a certain detachment from the immediate present, a capacity to shift attention to various aspects of a given circumstance—a capacity, in other words, to envision the circumstance's possibilities. Choice, decision, fully deliberate and volitional action, and self-direction in general are not conceivable in the absence of imagination in this sense. It is a simplification, but it is hardly an exaggeration, to say that the development of self-direction and individual autonomy is at the same time the development of the capacity for abstract thought.

One of the most striking evidences of this relationship is in the negative case. I am referring to the effects on psychological function of brain injury. Observation of brain-injured patients, for example, by Goldstein and Scheerer[4] clearly shows that the severe impairment of abstract thinking as a consequence of brain injury constitutes at the same time a remarkable destruction of volitional processes. The behavior of these patients is described as "will-less," as reduced to the automatic or habitual and to passive, reflexive reaction to the concrete and immediately apprehended present.

For instance, Goldstein's patients are unable to draw a map of their ward but can complete one if it is started for them. One patient is unable to set the hands of a clock at a given hour but can recognize the time when the clock is

[4]K. Goldstein and M. Scheerer, "Abstract and Concrete Behavior, An Experimental Study with Special Tests," *Psychological Monographs* (1941) 53:2.

presented. Another patient can continue counting or writing letters when the series is started for him, but cannot proceed spontaneously: "He is unable to initiate an action on his own. . . ."[5]

These patients have lost the capacity to detach their attention from what is immediately before them. They are, therefore, unable to plan, guide, or initiate an action toward an end that must be imagined. They are "stimulus bound."

Goldstein and Scheerer conclude:

From observation in normal as well as in pathological cases, there can be no doubt that a condition corresponding either to conscious will, or to the loss of it, exists. We need not speculate beyond this descriptive observation as to what kind of psychological "force" this conscious volition might represent. It suffices that this sort of act belongs to the functioning of the *normal* personality on the level of abstract behavior; that its presence or absence coincides with the presence or absence of the abstract attitude.[6]

Goldstein repeatedly emphasizes that the capacity for abstraction should not be regarded as a capacity of thought or of the intellect alone. It is, he insists, an "attitude," a "capacity level of the total personality." The full significance of this distinction is not, at least in my own experience, easy to grasp. In order to do so, I believe, one must understand that abstract thought and its opposite, stimulus-bound or concrete thought, actually imply different relationships between the individual and the external world—or, more exactly, between the individual and the (generally external) object of his interest. For example, these brain-damaged patients clearly lack a certain kind of detachment from the objects they deal with. They *see*

[5] Ibid., p. 5.
[6] Ibid., pp. 9–10.

the objects but cannot *examine* them. They react to the objects (in an automatic or a habitual way) but cannot *think* about them.

Another patient was well able to use eating utensils while eating, whereas given these objects outside of the eating situation, he produced only a jumble of senseless movements with them.[7]

The attitude of these patients toward the external world was not an objective one. In a certain sense, insofar as it would imply a sense of separateness from an objective world, they had no attitude *toward* the world at all. It was not objectified for them.

The absence of an objective sense of the external world makes impossible the imaginative manipulation of circumstances and the projection of possibilities that make up conscious aims and plans. Hence, the "concrete attitude" cannot give rise to consciously purposive, volitional action but allows only immediate, passive, or habitual reaction. One cannot imagine self-direction or volitional action in the absence of an objective relationship to the world.

Conversely, the "abstract attitude"—the capacity to regard a thing conceptually, as a member of a class or of various possible classes, and to consider it from various points of view, without regard for its incidental context—implies a detachment from that thing and an objective attitude toward it. Such an attitude toward what is external also implies a sense of the self's separateness from it and therefore an objective sense of the self. Such objective experience of the world permits one to imagine things in other than their existing contexts and to imagine oneself in other than one's present circumstances. It implies a sense of possibilities and ultimately of the possibilities of action.

[7]Ibid., p. 5.

I believe that the objectification of the world in this sense is more than a condition for self-direction: it makes self-directed action inevitable. Each developmental advance in the objectification of the world is associated with a corresponding advance in self-directedness and in the individual's autonomy. It appears, in fact, that the level of objectification of the world, on the one hand, and the level of self-directedness or autonomy, on the other, are different aspects of the individual's relationship with the external world at a given time.

Infancy and the Development of Intentionality

The newborn infant neither makes choices nor even takes action in the proper sense of the word. He simply reacts—reflexively, instinctively, often diffusely—to the "vital, global situation," in Heinz Werner's phrase.[8] Werner describes the immediacy of this earliest kind of action as follows:

There are no genuinely personal motives in primitive action. Primitive action is set in motion by vital drives on the one hand and by the concrete signals of the milieu on the other. . . . [The infant] moves, not because he is experiencing any form of aspiration, but rather because vital needs force him to move. . . .[9]

The infant does not initially have a sense of himself as separate from the external world. He does not have a sense, much less a concept, of an external or objective world nor, therefore, does he have a sense as such of his own actions or

---

[8]Heinz Werner, *Comparative Psychology of Mental Development* (Chicago: Follett, 1948), pp. 194–95.
[9]Ibid., pp. 194–95.

needs. Spitz[10] compares the quality of such undifferentiated subjective and sensory experience to the earliest visual experiences of adults who have been cured of lifelong blindness. These people are dazzled and at first are completely unable to distinguish visual forms from the dazzling sensory experience. One subject was initially unaware that these sensations were coming to her through her eyes.

Piaget points out that even the new infant's apparent recognition of an object is insufficient grounds for concluding that he actually has a sense of an external object:

It is not enough that a sensorial image be recognized when it reappears for it to constitute by itself an external object. Any subjective state can be recognized without being attributed to the action of objects independent of the ego. The newborn child who nurses recognizes the nipple by the combination of sucking and swallowing reflexes without making the nipple a thing. So also a month-old child can recognize certain visual images without, however, really exteriorizing them.[11]

Thus, Piaget suggests, the infant's smile, which later becomes a social response, is originally simply a reaction of pleasure occasioned by the recognition of a pleasing and familiar experience.

In general, according to Piaget, behavior in earliest infancy may outwardly resemble and suggest intentionality without actually having that significance.

When the child grasps an object in order to suck it, look at it, etc., he seems to differentiate the means from the ends and, consequently,

[10]Rene A. Spitz, *The First Year Of Life* (New York: International Universities Press, 1965), p. 55. See also M. von Senden, *Space and Sight: The Perception of Space and Shape in the Congenitally Blind before and after Operation* (London: Methuen, 1960).

[11]Piaget, quoted in J. H. Flavell, *The Developmental Psychology of Jean Piaget* (Princeton, N.J.: Van Nostrand, 1963), p. 96..

to set a goal in advance. But . . . nothing warrants attributing these distinctions to the subject's consciousness. Grasping in order to suck constitutes a single act in which the means and the end are one. . . . It is therefore the observer not the subject who makes [such] divisions [at this time].[12]

One cannot speak of genuine intentionality as long as the infant does not recognize a separation between himself and the external world, between his action and its object, or between his experience of an object and the object itself. The infant is still only reflexively or instinctively reactive. His "action" is immediate, without mediation; it is without intent and in that sense passive.

The emergence of intentionality—of action with a goal in mind—out of essentially passive, immediate reactiveness is too gradual to be marked with any precision. According to Piaget, reflexes gradually and imperceptibly become modified and, as it were, educated. Learning to suck the thumb is an example of this process. What were originally immediate reactions seem to acquire, through the experience of various environmental effects, the character or "feel" of action although still without a clearly imagined goal. For example, the infant, who is developing visual-grasping coordination, learns to grasp the rattle when—but only when—it is in visible proximity to his hand. Or the infant becomes interested in continuing or repeating the noise made by doing something with the rattle, but this interest must be triggered (in a way somewhat reminiscent of Goldstein and Scheerer's patients) by the adventitious presence of the rattle itself in the infant's hand.

Such action reflects a barely perceptible advance in intentionality beyond a reflexive reaction to a stimulus. Still, if we try to reconstruct the processes involved in it, even such barely

[12]Ibid., p. 111.

intentional action implies some recognition of that which was there and is now there again. The action does not, it is true, imply any clearly articulated or objective conception of an external "something." Yet it seems beyond doubt that the action marks an articulation of experience of the world sufficient at least to stir some kind of feeling of recognition of the rattle-in-hand. For only such recognition can kindle an interest not previously present and thus create the beginnings of self-directedness.

Recognitions occur to the infant as he, at first passively, accumulates experience of the environment, including repeated experience both of his own accidental activity and of such actions upon him as the ministrations of his mother. Such recognitions are bound to create new interests, new expectancies and anticipations, even if these are as yet not associated with any internal or imagined representation of the goal. The recognition of the rattle creates an interest in the rattle as an object out of what had been only an interest in a sensory experience. The rattle has become an attractive object, an object to be grasped. These beginnings of objectification do not so much change the infant's attitude toward the external world as create an attitude; it is not so much that his point of view is altered as that he begins to have a point of view.

It may be that a process of this sort occurs also in the early visual articulation of the external world—that is, in the development of active looking. Senden,[13] in the research previously mentioned, observed that initially perception of even the simplest forms was impossible for the newly seeing, previously blind people he studied, and was achieved only

[13]von Senden, *Space and Sight* [10].

after laborious teaching and visual guiding of the newly seeing student through the elementary visual forms. In this way, after repeated exposure, a certain level of elementary articulation was achieved. Senden found, however, that once this level was achieved, further progress in "learning to see" came rapidly, and the students' initial difficulty and resistance, sometimes so great as to cause them or their teacher to discontinue efforts altogether, tended to disappear. Such a process has sometimes been described as "learning to learn." In other words, the laborious acquisition of elementary perceptual articulations, once accomplished, alters the individual's visual relationship to the external world. Once such elementary recognitions are established, new visual interests are created. The acquisition of the elements of form perception then not only makes possible but also inevitable a new and more active kind of looking at the world because it has created new kinds of things to look at.

By the end of the first year, a "polarity between object and subject"—in Heinz Werner's phrase[14]—an attitude of interest and anticipation directed toward external things, an attitude of I-want-that or I-want-to-get-to-that, seems to be clearly established. By this time also a clear indication of intentionality appears in the form of instrumental action. The child is able —at first still requiring that the goal be visible—to push an obstacle away or to search for a means to reach it. The two developments are related. The possibility of such instrumental or mediating steps clearly indicates that the child has a goal in mind, as Flavell says, "prior to the consummatory response."[15]

The capacity to use action in this way, as a means to some-

[14]Werner, *Comparative Psychology* [8]
[15]Flavell, *Psychology of Piaget* [11], p. 111.

thing else, depends upon means and goal having become distinct from one another and upon the goal having become sufficiently distinct for its achievement to be anticipated, in however near a future, and however necessary the support of its visible presence. It implies, as Flavell says, that both means and end "have been pried loose from their original contexts."[16] The child has developed some awareness, out of further experience, of the object-ness of things, of their having an existence and being characterized by qualities that are independent of their present appearance, function, and relation to himself. At the same time, the child has achieved a certain detachment and sense of separateness from things—as Werner puts it, "a release from the domination of the concrete field."[17]

The beginnings of objectification of the world, therefore, have altered the child's relation to his environment, the nature of his interest in the environment, and his behavior toward the environment. To have a goal in mind prior to action is to regard the immediate vicinity with a new interest—the achievement of that goal. Hence, an interest in routes of action. In short, the objectification of the world, by bringing external goals into existence, transforms the child into an active goal-seeking individual.

By the same token, the limitations of the infant's objectification of the world define the formal limits of his action. As long as an object must be visible in order to prompt the infant's interest and purposive action, he is capable of action that is only simple, direct, and short-range. The existence of an objective goal has created a new impetus in the child to achieve that goal, and even a new interest in simple instrumentalities; but inasmuch as this goal has only a faint and unstable internal status, dependent actually on the object's external presence,

[16]Ibid., p. 111.
[17]Werner, *Comparative Psychology* [8], p. 192.

the impetus prompted by it has little flexibility and, as it were, little independent power.[18]

The essential condition for further significant advance in volitional action is the child's achievement of detached and durable internal representations of external reality, in particular of external goals.[19] Such a capacity means that, out of further and more varied experience, the child has achieved a more objective view of the world. He is more clearly aware of the independent existence of things and can now imagine them even when they are out of sight. This capacity also develops gradually. Piaget demonstrates, for example, that before the acquisition of language and the conceptual-symbolic representation of external reality, the child achieves a capacity for a primitive kind of internal representation, a "feeling" of imagined reality which is a product of the sensory-motor experience of that reality—a feeling that permits a degree of imaginative manipulation of events and a kind of sensory-motor

[18]This matter bears on an important point in psychoanalytic theory. In that theory, the development from an infantile immediacy of reaction to purposive, adaptive action, depends on the development of internal capacities for "delay" of tension discharge. It is through the emergence of internal tension-controlling structures, themselves reflecting and in a sense representing external conditions, that—in David Rapaport's term—increasingly "tamed" and adaptive forms of motivational tension develop ("The Conceptual Model of Psychoanalysis," in *The Collected Papers of David Rapaport,* Merton M. Gill, ed. [New York: Basic Books, 1967], pp. 405–31.) But the precise nature of these internal tension-controlling or delaying processes, and the manner in which they come into being, has never been entirely clear. The analysis that I have presented here suggests, on the other hand, that it is not the internalized capacity for delay that gives rise to the derivative, more adaptive motivation, but the other way around: it is the new form of motivation, the increasingly articulated aim, and increasingly clear anticipation of a goal, resulting from the objectification of the external world, that delays tension discharge. To the extent that a motivational tension has the form of a conscious aim and is directed toward an anticipated goal, delay, control, and tolerance of frustration become simply aspects of the process of anticipation, planning, and purposive action. On the other hand, to the extent that such a conscious aim is lacking and motivation consists only of an unarticulated need or tendency, delay or control is meaningless and impossible. See also Shapiro, *Neurotic Styles* (New York: Basic Books, 1965), p. 189.

[19]By "detached representation" I mean an image or idea that the child distinguishes from the object it represents.

"reflectiveness." Even such beginnings of the imaginative representation of things or events permit an expanded awareness of the world. The child is freed to some extent from the limitations of the present (which has been likened by Piaget to a slow-motion film in which each event can be linked only to those with which it is immediately involved). Thus, the child becomes increasingly aware of causal and temporal relations among events that to him previously were unrelated. In other words, the child's more detached, objective view is at the same time a wider one.

This achievement again significantly revises the child's relationship to his environment to a more active and directed one. He begins to reflect about the world, not only to experience it. His goals are more clearly articulated than they were before, and new areas of interest emerge. He has new possibilities of instrumental action, including the invention of new instrumental means; and action becomes both wider ranging and more flexible. Whereas the child's activity was previously limited to the pursuit of interesting things that happened to be present, he will now be interested as well in searching for what is not present and in rearranging his surroundings according to his liking.

"Willfulness" and the First Relations with Authority

The child's achievement of a certain capacity for volitional action leads directly to a new kind of relationship with adults. This relationship is a product of forces from two directions: the child wants to exercise his autonomy; and at the same time, the adults not only feel obliged to exercise certain constraints on this new activity but also see the opportunity to influence the child in new ways. Thus begins a complicated and close connection between the development of the internal processes of autonomy, on the one hand, and the child's relations with adult authority, on the other.

In earliest infancy no such relationship with authority exists. Adult authority as such has no meaning in the absence of self-direction. But from the earliest self-direction until the development of the internal processes of autonomy is complete —normally at the end of adolescence—and continuing through adult life in the case of certain kinds of psychopathology, the particular form and level of the individual's self-direction will determine, in part, the subjective significance to him of authority and the nature of his relationship with authority. There is in addition, of course, an effect in the opposite direction: the development of the child's autonomy will be affected by the nature of the adult authority the child encounters. The effects go in both directions in this close connection between the internal processes of autonomy and the individual's relations with external authority. Each is in various ways sensitive to the status of the other.

In the first real flush of autonomy, when the child has acquired a certain degree of muscular development and therefore a greater range of volitional activity and control, adults may begin to describe him as willful, stubborn, or difficult. Such descriptions reflect an adult point of view, not to say certain adult prejudices; in actual fact, it is not likely that the child, originally at least, is interested in contesting the parents' authority. The child simply wants to do what he wants to do. He is quite willing to do what he is supposed to do if he happens to want to do it, and may even at such times be described as surprisingly pliant. But just as his wanting to do what he is not supposed to do is not necessarily stubbornness, so his wanting to do what he is supposed to do is not necessarily pliancy: it may merely be coincidence. The child is simply interested in following his interests in his own way, sometimes in directions pointed by adults and sometimes not. Furthermore, since his activity is still quite unplanful, still with little sense of himself acting or about to act, the normal constraints of adult authority are likely to have only a concrete and present significance, without general—and often without lasting—meaning. The child has to be told again and again not to do this or that, and still he persists. Yet even this is not, originally at least, negativism or even, properly speaking, willfulness. It is merely determination. There is no doubt that the child can be forced into contest with adult authority or, perhaps more accurately, with superior adult power. There is no doubt, in other words, that he can be made to react to the fact, even if he is not aware of it, that more may be involved in continual prohibitions and constraints than the doing or not doing of particular things— namely the question, Who is to be in charge of what he does?

The appearance of autonomous activity in the child prompts adults to new kinds of constraints and a new exercise of authority for several reasons. Partly, of course, this is simply a matter of inevitable conflicts between the more assertive activity of the child and the practical requirements and regulations of the household and of safety. From the first signs of the child's capacity for self-direction and volitional control, however, the opportunity presents itself for the adult to exercise a more durable and extensive influence on the child's behavior than was previously possible. The appearance of the child's will presents the adult with the opportunity to influence the child's will. A conspicuous example of this is toilet training.

With the development of the muscular system and of more solid stool, the child becomes aware of his own bowel movements. The bowel movement, in other words, becomes objectified for him; and thus, volitional control of it begins. Parents realize this stage has been reached when the child begins to signal or to give some other evidence of an approaching bowel movement. It is at this point usually that they begin to exercise their influence or their authority, if only to indicate for the child the new aim of using the toilet or potty, giving it a name, and so on, to encourage volitional control.

In this way, volitional control is gradually extended to an originally wholly reflexive and immediate muscular reaction, and this extension of autonomy occurs, significantly, to a greater or lesser extent under the auspices of conscious parental influence or authority. There is every evidence, given parents reasonably sensitive to and respectful of the child's own will and capacity, that this development can take place smoothly and without special difficulties. But we know that it presents various possibilities of interference with the exercise of the child's autonomy and hence with his normal development. It is well known, for example, that toilet training can become an arena for a contest of wills, or even for a contest between the will of the adult and the physiology of the child. It is not difficult to identify, retrospectively, later distortions of autonomy as outcomes of this encounter with coercive authority: anxious obedience or a readiness to submit or surrender, a reflexive and angry resistance to authority and sensitivity to the possibility of coercion, and, perhaps above all, a rigid volitional control which, like a puppet government, appears to be autonomous but actually relies on an awareness of superior authority. But, actually, even at this early age, toilet training is not the child's only encounter with adult authority. For, as the child gives evidence of increasing self-direction, not to speak of "willfulness," adults will attempt to influence his will in many areas, not only for the purpose of affecting his present behavior but also to affect his character, to inculcate general constraints, standards, moral prohibitions, and so on. Furthermore, the same parental attitudes that are reflected in toilet training are likely to be reflected in other areas, and the child's experience of that general form of adult authority—coercive, for example —seems more likely to be responsible for lasting distortions of autonomy than any specific encounter with such authority.

To cite an extreme example, the fanatical father of the paranoid schizophrenic, Schreber, who became the subject of Freud's famous study,[20] apparently recommended beginning when the child was two with the program of rigid training, including orthopedic apparatus, strictly regulated behavior, physical training, precise schedules, and so on, which he advocated to guarantee upright posture and upright character.[21]

In my opinion, we cannot yet identify with confidence the precise effects on the development of autonomy of the earliest encounters with various forms of adult authority or coercion, except perhaps in such exceptional cases. The discovery of early prototypes for more complex adult states of mind is easy enough: the biographer can always find that the child Einstein was already thinking about something that resembled relativity. But the attempt to understand adult pathology in terms of early prototypes invariably must rest on analogies, because the early prototype actually does not contain many of the specific features of the adult pathology that depend on later developments. The identification of earlier, less differentiated tendencies with later, more differentiated conditions, of which they

[20]Sigmund Freud, "Psychoanalytical Notes Upon an Autobiographical Account of a Case of Paranoia," *Collected Papers*, vol. III (London: Hogarth Press and Institute of Psychoanalysis, 1949), pp. 387–470.
[21]See William G. Niederland, *The Schreber Case: Psychoanalytic Profile of a Paranoid Personality* (New York: Quadrangle, 1974).

may be genuine *sources,* only obscures, in the final analysis, their actual developmental relationship.

As the child's capacity for self-direction continues to develop and his activities become more planned, complicated, and extensive, the place of adult authority and prestige in his life does not diminish, and will not for some time to come. On the contrary, the domain of influence of that authority enlarges with the extension of the child's own capacity, activity, and interests. The way things are to be done or not done, the definition of what should be done, and what should not, of what is good, and what is bad—all of these must at first rely on or issue from adults. The morality of the child develops out of this respect for parental authority; and his earliest moral judgments are based, according to Piaget's findings, on a naïve and literal acceptance of adult authority as absolute—a "moral realism," as Piaget calls it. He describes this morality as a morality of constraint: "Right is to obey the will of the adult; wrong is to have a will of one's own."[22] Such a morality of constraint is not necessarily the product of coercive adult authority. It seems, rather, to be simply where moral judgment must begin, and adult constraints and influences provide, in this as in other matters, some of the materials for the child's own developing will and judgment.

Further Development of Objectiveness

The continued development of the child's thinking and objectiveness continues to revise his relationship to his environment. He has been transformed from one who is helplessly

[22]Jean Piaget, *The Moral Judgment of the Child* (Glencoe, Ill.: Free Press, n.d.) p. 193.

reactive to his environment into one who actively pursues his own aims within that environment. Nevertheless, his activities and his aims remain limited essentially to what he has already experienced in that environment, and to what it appears in an immediate way to offer him. The further development of thought, particularly the further development of the capacity for symbolization of external reality, will free him from the limitations of his circumstances and of his own actual experience. It will permit him an awareness of external reality which is far more extensive, more complicated, and deeper than actual experience can possibly provide. Through conceptual language, it will bring him into contact, in Piaget's words, with "an already prepared system of ideas, classifications, relations —in short, an inexhaustible stock of concepts."[23] The further development of thought will therefore, ultimately endow him with great power to *affect* his environment.

The child's earliest internal representations of external reality are concrete, subjective, and personal. They are recollections of circumstance and action, dominated by what is immediately striking and uninformed by other perspectives. The child pictures things as he pictures them, in ways that strike him according to his subjective standpoint at the time. He is not sufficiently detached from such representations to examine them, turn them over in his mind, think about his own thoughts. It is apparent that such representations can guide actions, but only very simple actions, hardly different from what the child has already experienced and essentially limited to trial and error.

As the child approaches and enters school age, his ideas of things become less personal, less bound to his own experience of them, more objectively classified, or—as Richmond says—

[23]Quoted in P. G. Richmond, *An Introduction to Piaget* (New York: Basic Books, Harper Torchbooks, 1970), p. 84.

ordered "more in accord with the conceptual nature of language."[24] The child's thinking starts to become more flexible, his attention more mobile: that is, he becomes aware of different points of view than his own and gradually able to direct his attention to various aspects of his picture of a situation, to imagine it from other perspectives or from the point of view of other relations. Flavell points out an interesting manifestation of this increased flexibility—that from about the age of four or five the child becomes more testable: he becomes able to direct his attention according to instructions or upon request.[25]

It gradually, and then increasingly, becomes possible for the child to manipulate ideas of things. It becomes possible for him to shift his perspective on things more easily. He achieves a more abstract awareness of things: that is to say, that out of the conceptual articulations of language, as a result of contact with the viewpoints of others, out of further direct experience, and so on, he comes to perceive things in classes, to realize what is unvarying and essential from a given point of view and what is contingent and inessential.

He becomes aware also, therefore, of certain logical relations among things. In general, a shift is under way from a way of thinking about things that is "intuitive"—that is, largely dependent upon how things immediately look, and hence limited to a single viewpoint or an apparent relation—to thinking that is based on an awareness of the logical relations among things or classes of things. This kind of thinking, which, in Piaget's view, becomes increasingly well established and complex through middle childhood, frees the child's ideas from the limitations of what he concretely perceives. His ideas can extend now to the possible.

[24]Ibid., p. 36.
[25]Flavell, *Psychology of Piaget* [11], p. 162.

Such a development might be described in a number of ways. Piaget speaks of continually diminished egocentricity, or subjectiveness. It can as well be described as continually increasing in its objectiveness, in its detached and abstract attitude toward the world. It is as though—through experience, the conceptual articulations of language, contact with the viewpoints of others—an objective, wider world continues to materialize for the child. His view comes to be less dominated by his immediate interests and circumstances and to allow recognition of the various relations among things. In turn, such a view creates new possibilities for his interest, changes his relation to the world, once again, to a more active one and changes him into a more planful and deliberate individual.

Let me return to a first principle: the recognition of a new aspect of a thing can bring into being a relation to that thing which did not exist before. The child learns that the small, shiny glass objects that he has handled are called marbles, and that certain games can be played with them. A new object—marbles—has been created. At the same stroke, a new subject —a marble player—has come into being. In this way, each recognition of a new aspect of a thing or an event may create not only a new object but also a newly active subject. Similarly, each stage of further objectification of the world—by extending the child's interests, by creating new, more complicated, more distant aims, and by opening new possibilities of activity —creates a more actively and consciously directed individual, a child who will direct himself according to those more complicated, more distant purposes: in other words, a more autonomous child.

Thus, with the achievement of a more detached and abstract awareness of the world, of some of the world's possibilities beyond the apparent, a newly reflective child comes into being. He has a new curiosity and, for example, new interests in how things work. In his play, he becomes more interested in imitating reality, in doing things that work, and so forth. He becomes, if all goes well, eager to learn and become competent in doing things. His action becomes more planned and deliberate. And as his action becomes more reflective and deliberate, he becomes more conscious of action itself, more self-aware.

Further Relations with Adult Authority—
Self-respect and Feelings of Inferiority

The child's relations with adult authority alter significantly after the early period of so-called willfulness or resistance. Approximately from the age of three, children are described as more "agreeable," easier to lead, and the like; and the particular kind of friction that is characteristic of the earlier period diminishes on the whole. How is one to account for this diminished resistance of the child to what might objectively seem to be innumerable infringements on his autonomy by adult authority—parents and, later, teachers—just when the range of his activity and competency and the extent of his self-direction are rapidly expanding? In some cases and in some settings, perhaps, it could be said that that early willfulness has simply been subdued. Normally these children do not look subdued, however; they look enthusiastic. If their resistance to adult authority has diminished, it is apparently because the direction of their interests has changed—as well as their relation to and picture of adult authority.

The further development of a more objective, less egocentric picture of the world implies the development of a somewhat more objective, less egocentric picture of adults. This is to say that the child comes to perceive and to admire the competency and authority of adults, parents principally, which before he had only experienced (as subject or beneficiary) and reacted to. Children then want to acquire that competency. They imitate the admired adults and want to be like them. The earlier conflict with adult authority is for the time being replaced by a coincidence of interests of child and adult: the child is eager to learn, the adult world is eager to teach. The child's admiration of, and identification with, the adult nullifies—let me say, tends to nullify—the conflict between them otherwise inherent in the imposition of adult constraints and authority.

During this period, therefore, the authority of adults as teachers and models is very great. Ideas and attitudes stamped by the adults' prestige, as well as skills and competencies learned from adults, contribute to the child's own judgment and competency and, thus, ultimately to his autonomy. An important, if special, case of this process is described by Piaget in his studies of the development of moral judgment. Such judgment begins with the child's literal acceptance of the moral authority of adult constraints and the reification of these into absolute law: wrong is what is prohibited and punishable by adults. Between this stage and the achievement of an autonomous moral judgment—which, if it is achieved at all, reflects the individual's own social experience and intelligence—is an interesting intermediate stage. In this stage, adult authority has become translated into rules and regulations that, while retaining the subjective quality of authoritative imperatives, are interpreted and applied by the child as his own, to particular situations. "At a given moment the child thinks that lies are bad in themselves and that, even if they are not punished, one ought not to lie."[26] This principle, however, is still experienced

[26]Jean Piaget, *The Moral Judgment of the Child* (Glencoe, Ill.: Free Press, n.d.), p. 194.

as an authoritative rule laid down by the adult and not as an intrinsic ideal of social relations.

The moral imperatives of adult authority become in this gradual way internalized and contribute materials and form to the child's own judgment, perhaps even a sense of the authority of his own judgment. On the other hand, insofar as this judgment relies on an authoritative rule or directive, derives its weight from adult authority, and reflects the child's identification with that authority, it is not an independent judgment but, as it were, a borrowed one, and any sense of personal authority it may offer is borrowed authority. A judgment of this kind is, in effect, a dogma. Furthermore, precisely because such a judgment relies subjectively on the superior authority of the adult, it introduces a schism into the mind of the child: on the one hand, the child identifies with adult constraint; on the other, it is not completely his own, and he may even be the object of that constraint. This schism has far-reaching consequences: the identification with the adult that tends to nullify the child's conflict with adult authority, at the same time introduces an internal version of that conflict into the mind of the child.

Robert W. White says that "identification can be said to serve as an imaginative short cut to the mastery of complex adult patterns of behavior."[27] Clearly, identification with adult figures is in this sense not only an inevitable but also an essential developmental process, guiding the child, providing transitional direction and support on the way to the development of his own authority and his own views and judgments. It is not difficult to imagine, however, that if this development does not proceed well, such an identification with various figures of real

[27]Robert W. White, "Ego and Reality in Psychoanalytic Theory: A Proposal Regarding Independent Ego Energies," *Psychological Issues*, vol. III/3, Monograph 11, p. 114.

or imagined superior authority and competence may become a permanent characteristic of the adult. I shall try to show in the following chapters that an identification of this sort does, in fact, figure importantly in the psychology of rigid character.

It is easy to observe a child's satisfaction and pride in learning things and doing things effectively. The experience seems to nourish self-confidence and self-esteem. It seems reasonable to suppose, therefore, that such experience, cumulatively, is an important source not only of a sense of competence, effectiveness, or mastery but also ultimately, of a sense of personal weight and authority—in other words, of self-respect. White regards such experience of efficacy, as he calls it, as being the "taproot" of self-esteem (which he means essentially in the sense of self-respect). He says: "Understanding self-esteem means understanding the history of action and its consequences."[28] In this statement, he refers to the child's experiences of efficacy and competence in the course of development: manipulative activity, mastery of language, schoolwork, social relations, and so on. It is an important and plausible assertion because it relates self-esteem to the child's actual experience of himself, as opposed to fantasy or the social response to him.

Still, it seems advisable to be cautious in extrapolating this relationship. There are certain problems in connection with it and certain aspects of it are not altogether clear. As far as adults are concerned at least, we are inclined to think that a self-esteem or self-respect that depends on demonstrated competency and achievement, on what the individual can do or has done, is not a secure or well-established self-esteem or self-respect at all. In other words, we think of self-esteem or self-

[28]Ibid., p. 134.

respect as referring to more intrinsic characteristics of the person than his achievement or his competency. Furthermore, the meaning of "self-esteem" itself, even in White's careful usage, is by no means unambiguous, and its ambiguity may be related to the same problem. Does self-esteem or self-respect consist of relatively stable feelings of self-appreciation, as in recognition of successful performance? Or do we mean by self-esteem or self-respect an unself-conscious quality of subjective experience, a sense of personal weight or authority, that is only implied in the willingness to trust one's own experience and perception of things, to make one's own judgments, to follow one's own interests and aims, and to exercise what competency one has? Still further, if it is true that self-esteem or self-respect is nourished by experiences of effective activity, would it be reasonable to assume that feelings of inferiority or insufficiency grow out of the unsuccessful ventures of childhood? If that were so, it might be difficult to explain why all children do not suffer much more acutely than they do from such feelings.

It seems doubtful that—aside from their simulations in certain kinds of psychopathology—conscious, lasting positive feelings of self-esteem or self-respect as such are an important part of normal subjective life. We experience, of course, transient feelings of pride and satisfaction in connection with particular achievements or recognition, but the closest approximations we know of lasting or continual self-appreciation are easily recognized as compensatory efforts, unconvincing and only half-believed by the subjects themselves. Actually, those individuals whom we describe as self-confident or possessed of self-respect seem to be characterized not so much by a feeling of esteem for themselves as by an absence of concern with themselves.

This conclusion is confirmed by observation of patients who

are successfully treated in psychotherapy. In these people, one can observe a low self-esteem or feeling of inferiority gradually being replaced not by an equally self-conscious pride or self-appreciation but by a diminished interest in the matter. They simply become less concerned with measuring themselves and more interested in activity and life. Altogether, it appears that self-esteem or self-respect is much like the sense of physical well-being or health: it is experienced as such on occasion, but primarily it is reflected in an absence of painful or uncomfortable self-awareness and in a readiness for activity—meaning particularly, in this connection, judgments, decisions, and, in general, following one's own lights.[29]

Self-esteem or, as I prefer, self-respect is comparable to physical well-being in another sense. The state of health has its physiology, just as disease does; but there is a sense in which health or the feeling of well-being, unlike disease, does not require explanation. We do not have to explain by the presence of special conditions why someone does not have a stomach-ache or an ulcer. We take that as expected, as understood by the physiology of the human being in general. Only disease must be explained by the presence of special conditions. The same thing, I believe, can be said of self-respect as compared with, for example, feelings of inferiority: the development of self-respect can be understood as a reflection of normal growth and the normal development of autonomy in general; it is not directly dependent on special conditions of competence, achievement, or success.

It is, I think, not only that one wishes it to be so, but that experience demonstrates that self-respect or feelings of inferi-

[29]As it pertains to the developing self-esteem of children, this conclusion is consistent with Erikson's picture of the alternative ego qualities of the latency child: not as self-esteem versus a sense of inferiority, but as *industry* versus a sense of inferiority (*Childhood and Society* [2]). [New York: W. W. Norton, 1950]).

ority can be found in individuals of all levels of intelligence, all degrees of competence and achievement, and even among severely limited and handicapped individuals who are well aware of their limitations and handicaps. If effective, competent activity is a direct and principal source of self-respect, the reason is not obvious why, to put the matter simply, self-respect should not be largely the possession of the brightest, the most competent, the most successful.

We have seen that as the child develops, his behavior is continuously less passively and immediately reactive to the environment, progressively more actively directed according to his own plans. In a manner of speaking, he carries more weight in the determination of his behavior. It is, in my opinion, primarily this general development of the child's autonomy, in which activity will have played its part, rather than the direct experience of effective action, that is the basis of a developing sense of personal significance, of "being somebody," and ultimately of personal authority and self-respect. The child feels more significant because he has actually become so, not merely in the sense of being technically competent but in the deeper and more intrinsic sense of becoming an independent agent in the world. Competent action, achievements, and success are particular external manifestations of this development and, therefore, may and often do provide external confirmations, objective proofs, of one's significance and right to self-respect, especially where self-respect is weak or insecure. But if the development of autonomy has gone well, self-respect will not depend primarily on what one can do or how well one does it, will not require special justification, but will simply reflect what one is or is becoming—an autonomous human being.

It would be mistaken also, if this reasoning is correct, to draw the conclusion that feelings of inferiority derive in a direct way from actual deficiencies or limitations of competency. It seems rather that individuals whose self-respect is already uncertain endow various deficiencies or limitations with a profound and general significance, as though these were measures of their essential worth. The specific focus of such concerns is likely to change from time to time or even frequently: school or career failures, physical weakness, inadequate sexual performance, and so on. It is not unusual either for conspicuously competent and successful individuals to regard particular deficiencies as evidence of essential inferiority. On the other hand, when those—perhaps children especially—who are not already occupied by feelings of inferiority, fail in something that they would like to accomplish—provided that the matter is not endowed with great significance by others—it seems that they accept failure with regret or disappointment as a particular limitation, sometimes with a sense that it may only be temporary and in any case without general significance for their essential quality. From that standpoint, even severe limitations are not necessarily mortifying.

This acceptance is evident even in the following case recalled from childhood by a man diagnosed as retarded:

I kind of stood in the background—I kind of knew that I was different—I knew that I had a problem, but when you're young you don't think of it as a problem. A lot of people are like I was. The problem is getting labeled as being something. . . . I liked camp. The staff and counselors were good. I had this thing with my legs. They weren't very strong. When I fell back from the group on a hike I was light enough so that they could give me a ride on their backs. . . . I was glad that I was light because it was easier for them. I needed help and they helped. . . . I didn't mind being carried. . . . The important thing was that I was there.[30]

---

[30]Robert Bogdan and Steven Taylor, "The Judged, Not the Judges: An Insider's View of Mental Retardation," *American Psychologist*, January 1976, p. 48.

Feelings of inferiority imply not merely actual insufficiencies, which, after all are a central part of every child's life, but an awareness of standards that give such limitations a significance they otherwise would not have. In one form or another, a sense of insignificance or inferiority is probably a part of all neurosis. All neurosis involves some impairment of autonomy and, therefore, some impairment of self-respect. But in one form particularly, concerns with, and feelings of, inferiority are acute and preoccupying, sometimes even obsessive. To feel inferior in this sense is to live with images or ideas of what one should be, and to regard and measure oneself continually according to them. It is such feelings of inferiority, I believe, that constitute a conspicuous symptom.

In these people, apparently, the kind of subjective schism, the duality of attitude, that originates in the child's emulation of and identification with admired, or at any rate impressive, adults is prolonged and even intensified. It seems paradoxical, I realize, to assert that the child's emulation of adults should result in the gap between them becoming a permanent part of his subjective life. Yet that emulation is, after all, founded on the gap between inferior and superior. The child's aim in emulating adults is to close that gap, but he cannot, in actual fact, become what he is not. In this sense, the process of identification can never be completely successful. As the normal child grows, experiencing his own autonomy and his own significance, his interest in emulating adults diminishes, leaving those traits and influences that have taken root in the child's own personality.

When all has not gone well, however, development may take a different turn. The individual may continue to live under the sway of images of superior figures and figures of superior authority and may, in the presence of such largeness and authority, continue to feel small and insignificant. Self-respect, for him, is contingent on his likeness to these figures; he continues to emulate them, to attempt to "live up to" them, to regard himself and measure himself according to them—and continually, inevitably, he falls short. Thus, he does not simply feel small: he is oppressed by a continual consciousness of himself as small.

Adolescence and the Awareness of Autonomy

Adolescents are often said to be egocentric; but if they are more so than younger children, it is in the sense of being more conscious of and concerned with themselves. In the other sense of egocentricity—subjectiveness—they are certainly less egocentric. If they are more aware of themselves, they are also more aware of the world outside of themselves, beyond their own surroundings of family and school. Both of these kinds of awareness actually reflect a more detached and more objective point of view.

Mental development, in Piaget's general sense of intelligence, essentially reaches maturity in adolescence. According to Piaget, adolescents are capable of reasoning abstractly not only about things but also about ideas and relations among things. Just as in childhood things were "pried loose" from their existing contexts, so now in adolescence abstract relations are "pried loose" from their existing contexts. Various points of view, various aspects of things, are recognized for what they are. Ideas, such as "right" and "wrong" become objectified, objects of attention, and invite reflection—that is, "actions" of thought—upon them.

To be able thus to reflect on abstract ideas, on relations

among things, and on various points of view is to be able to regard things as they are as conditional. Such capacities, in other words, extend and liberate the imagination. Orders of possibilities and hypothetical conditions are opened; and present actual conditions—how things are right now—become, as Piaget says, only special cases of the possible.[31] Hence the imaginative and abstract interests of adolescents in the future, in society and social change, in ideology, justice, science— determined, of course, by their access to educational opportunity, imaginative technology, science fiction, and so on. All these abstract and imaginative interests reflect a more detached and a wider view of the world, a view from which the adolescent can consider not only things but also ideas about things, a more relativistic view from which many previously accepted notions will appear to him as mere prejudices. Such a wider view will also affect the picture of his immediate surroundings: they become somewhat diminished. Parents, family, home, neighborhood, even society are reduced from their status of the way things are and must be to the status of the way these particular things happen to be at present. At the same time, adolescents have a new consciousness of themselves, a more detached sense of their separate existence, and a more objective awareness of their situation, including, of course, an awareness of their approaching parity with the adult world.

This wider and more detached view, coinciding with physical and sexual maturation and great vitality, once again brings into being a more active and purposeful and, now, also, more consciously self-directing, individual. Adolescents are interested in doing new independent things—working, traveling, driving—and especially in doing things, and doing them in

[31]Flavell, *Psychology of Piaget* [11], pp. 204 ff.

ways, that they, or those they designate, have chosen. They, especially the most conscientious among them, may see things wrong with, and want to change, many of their circumstances, some of their existing relationships, the social order, themselves. They may not only imagine achievements and, if society permits, careers but also experiment with images of themselves as though deciding, not just what to do, but "what to be."

The dialectics of the relationship with adult authority reaches another stage. The potentialities of the child's reliance on adults, or at least on his parents, as teachers and models are in large measure achieved; and this achievement, in the form of adolescence, makes it more or less inevitable that he will contest the remaining constraints of adult authority. The earlier relationship of unequal rank—of "unilateral respect" for the parents, as Piaget puts it—is largely repudiated. The essential condition for its acceptance, the unquestioned superiority of adult authority and of the adult as teacher and model, no longer exists. For the adolescent's awareness of himself as a near-adult with his own ideas has given him a tentative respect for his own authority while at the same time he sees his parents more objectively, diminished to the size of other human beings.

The adolescent objection to adult constraints, however, has a different form from the willfulness of early childhood. It is not simply the early contest over the particular behavior of the child or particular constraints of the parent reproduced on a larger scale; although such factors are, it is true, usually present, as in conflicts between the immoderate and idealistic inclinations of the one and the cautiousness and moderation of the other. But there is also a more intrinsic issue between them. Adolescents are concerned with the right, in principle, to hold their own views, to follow their own lights, to be in charge of themselves. They are explicitly and consciously aware of and concerned with the matter of autonomy or self-determination itself, which in the circumstances necessarily involves the recognition of their rights by adults. Adolescents insist on privacy, freedom from intrusion, at least from intrusion by parents, and an independent domain. They want freedom of movement. They demand that their ideas be treated respectfully and their votes fully counted. In short, the adolescent's awareness of his own near-parity with the adult world and his tentative sense of personal authority generate an insistence on the right to exercise that personal authority.

In general, adolescence is full of exaggerated willfulness, defensiveness, and other symptoms of an unsteady, self-conscious, and sometimes simply artificial assertion of autonomy and personal authority. These symptoms are both of a sort that involves relations with authority and of a sort that involves more strictly internal processes. For example, often adolescents are pridefully, defensively sensitive to condescension or disrespect, especially from adults, or resentfully preoccupied with adult constraints, or they may repudiate familiar adult expectations and instructions while embracing exotic ones. Acute feelings of inferiority may intermittently be denied by arrogance; uncertainty may be covered by dogmatism. The adolescent may suffer the struggles of decision I have referred to—what "to be"—as well as ones of conscience, of self-control or "will power." The form and extent of some of these symptoms are likely to reflect social conditions as much as personal ones. For example, adolescent assertiveness can be expected to take more cynical or destructive forms where society offers no means for effecting, and places no value on, adolescent ambitions and ideals.[32]

The psychopathology of adolescence should not be regarded

[32]On the subject of adolescence and society, see Erik H. Erikson, *Identity, Youth and Crisis* (New York: W. W. Norton, 1968).

as equivalent, especially in prognostic significance, to the adult psychiatric conditions it may in some respects resemble[33]— this is especially clear in connection with such symptoms, or manifestations, as I have mentioned. They may resemble adult pathologies of autonomy—such as obsessional, compulsive, and even paranoid conditions—but these adolescent reactions and concerns may only be the inherently transient signs of a developmental process, the maturing of autonomy, and that only under particular external conditions. It is often easy to observe that as autonomy and self-respect become more securely established, exaggerated and self-conscious expressions of them diminish or disappear. On the other hand, it is also true that the conditions may now exist for more lasting pathology of autonomy, as in the varieties of rigid character.

[33]Ibid., p. 17.

Chapter 3

Rigid Character

I HAVE DESCRIBED several kinds of neurotic conditions and tendencies—obsessive-compulsive and paranoid conditions, sadistic and masochistic tendencies—as manifestations of rigid character. Before considering each of these conditions and tendencies in detail, the general description of rigid character and its implication of common understanding warrant some further explanation. For the time being, it will be convenient to refer primarily to the more inclusive obsessive-compulsive and paranoid conditions. Of course, all such psychiatric or psychological categories and generalizations are loose: no one is totally described by them and no one will find their description totally inapplicable to himself.

The individuals I will discuss are characterized by an exaggerated and tense deliberateness of behavior. Areas of life that are normally comparatively spontaneous, decisions that normally require only quick consideration—whether to go to the movies, how to spend an afternoon off—become matters of serious deliberation, often full of complex purposes.

The behavior of such a person may be almost continuously purposeful, aimed at getting somewhere, at achieving a result in the form of a product or at least the furthering of a plan. He does little for its own sake. This purposiveness may become very intense: careful, determined, tense, with his attention fixed on aims, although in certain cases it may include the effort to appear casual or offhand. It is a purposiveness that does not brook deviation or distraction. Hence one calls it rigid.

Such a continuously deliberate, purposive, and tense self-direction involves a special kind of self-awareness or self-consciousness. Rigid people direct themselves with a greater and more extensive awareness than others have of what they are doing, and how they are doing it. They do not forget themselves or lose themselves. In some cases even gestures—a handshake, a manner of walking—may be deliberate, aimed at achieving an effect, or avoiding an effect. Consequently, their behavior is not only deliberate but often stilted and artificial.

Among people of rigid character, autonomy itself is a matter of preoccupation and concern. These people are concerned with the issue of "giving in." The paranoid person is on guard against being pushed around, taken advantage of, or tricked. The compulsive person is concerned with "giving in" to temptation, to laziness, or to his emotions. Both types of rigid character must continually reinforce their sense of mastery: the paranoid person, by being "on top of" his circumstances, anticipating all threatening possibilities; the compulsive person, by exercising "will power" and by activeness, doing and accomplishing. Each has a special respect for "strength" and an abhorrence of "weakness," meaning primarily strength or weakness of will. In each of these matters, of course, the more rigid paranoid individual exceeds the comparatively less rigid compulsive person in the intensity of his concern.

It is clear that these people are engaged in a special and peculiar struggle for mastery of themselves, that autonomy involves a special kind of effort for them, and, further, one may assume that their rigidity is the outcome of this effort and the solution of this struggle. All that may be obvious. What is not obvious is the reason for such a struggle—the reason, for example, for such abhorrence of "weakness," "giving in," or relaxation of deliberate or willful self-direction or, to put the matter another way, the significance such a relaxation or "weakness" of the will may have for the individual.

I have already alluded to what appears to be the first significance of "weakness" to the rigid individual. It is implied in the meaning of "strength": the capacity to struggle against, resist, and overcome one's own feelings, to resist temptation, to resist doing what one actually wants to do or desires. Weakness, "giving in" to oneself, "losing control," and lack of "will," therefore, mean to do what one wants to do but should not do. The rigid person, in other words, experiences himself as having weakness of will or of self-control when his wish and intention are contrary to the directives of that will. To be more exact: the rigid person experiences weakness of self-control when the directives of his will, which he identifies as his wish, are contrary to his *actual but unrecognized* wish and intention.

Let me give an example from psychotherapy. A twenty-four-year-old woman, recently disappointed in a love affair, had for some time spoken of her determination to move to another city in order "to get a fresh start." Despite repeated and emphatic declarations of her intention and decision to make this move, she had not taken any practical steps toward it. The following

is a highly condensed account of an occasion when she came
to her therapy hour looking gloomy and quite upset about her
weakness of will in this matter:

PATIENT: What's the matter with me! I want to move, but I can't
seem to get started! It's nothing but inertia! Typical of me. . . . That's
the way I live my life, by inertia! Not doing what I really want to do!
THERAPIST: Usually people don't have to overcome so much inertia
to do what they really want to do. As a matter of fact, when they're
that eager, it's hard to hold them back.
PATIENT: Well, it's not exactly that I'm eager. But I know that I
would like it in the long run.
THERAPIST: Evidently the short run looks bad.
PATIENT: But I know it would be good for me!
THERAPIST: That's quite different from *wanting* to do it.
PATIENT: Whether I want to do it or I don't want to do it, I should
do it! I have to learn to become independent! I have to go some place
where I can't call on people all the time, where there's nobody to go
to, where I will have to take care of myself because I don't know a
soul and I will either sink or swim!
THERAPIST: I see why you're not rushing off to do it.
PATIENT: It would be horrible! [*She bursts into tears.*]

What—from her determined and moralistic standpoint—
this woman experienced as an inexplicable and disturbing failure of will, as "inertia" or inability to do what she "really
wanted" to do, actually was her strong desire not to do it at all.
She thought she *should* do it and *believed* that she wanted to
do it, but in fact she did not. What she experienced as weakness of will ("inertia") was actually an unrecognized contrary
inclination.

The process through which a motivation contrary to the
directives of will is transformed, in subjective experience, into
a sense of weakness of will or even, in some instances, one of
"losing control" reflects the effects on experience of fixed and

intensely prejudiced expectations. It happens regularly that, in their purposiveness and determination, rigid individuals mis-identify what they want, what they intend, and even what they believe. They mistake what they think they should want for what they actually do want, what they think should be their intentions for actual intentions, ideas that they think they should believe for convictions. The rigid person imagines that he wants to move, for example, like my patient; that he is convinced of the necessity for it and that he intends to do so when actually he only thinks he should be convinced and should do it and does not want or intend to move at all. He identifies certain imperatives of his "will" as his wish and he often expresses a supposed wish—"I want to move!" "I know it would be good for me!"—in the imperative style of will and, with the prejudice that such will entails, does not recognize contrary motivations as such, but experiences them only as laziness, inertia, or lack of discipline.

The authority of the rigid person's will, therefore, estranges him from his own feelings and motivations. Originally, it must have been the other way around: the directives and the author-ity now represented by that will were alien, imposed from the outside. This authority can only have originated in the child's relationship to the superior authority of the adult. The rigid person, however, has not internalized the aims, standards, and prohibitions of adult authority in the ordinary sense; the prob-lem is precisely that he imposes upon himself aims and pur-poses that have not been completely or satisfactorily internal-ized, that have not become his own. They have not completely "taken." If they had, the "strength," the "will power," the rigidity would not be necessary. On the other hand, internaliza-tion of some sort has surely occurred. Even if it is true that the rigid person lives under the authority of his will, it is also true that he himself imposes that authority, that he respects it, identifies its aims and purposes as his own, and guards them even against his own feelings.

On the basis of this picture, we may surmise the nature of that internalization and the significance and origins of that will. The rigid person, it appears, continues to emulate and to identify himself with images of superior authority derived from the child's image of the superior authority of the adult. The rigid person's will is the product of that emulation and identification. As I shall discuss in more detail in the following chapters, this hypothesis will help to explain many of the traits frequently found in persons of rigid character: for example, their pompousness and artificial air of authority, their affinity for dogma, their stiff and defensive pridefulness, and also their underlying sense of shame and inferiority. Here, however, I should like to show how such a relationship with superior authority can further clarify certain fundamental aspects of rigid self-direction, particularly its special relation to the external world.

The exaggerated forms of rigid behavior—its exaggerated deliberateness and purposiveness—make it difficult to avoid the notion that rigidity is a development that has somehow gone too far. In some sense, the deliberateness of the rigid person may easily appear to be the result of an overdevelopment of volitional direction and control and the overdevelopment of a detached and objective attitude—the opposite extreme of the subjectivity, the immediacy, and the passivity of reaction of early childhood. In fact, however, the condition of rigidity reflects not so much an overdevelopment of volitional direction and control as a miscarriage of that development. Flexibility—not rigidity—of behavior stands at the opposite pole from the immediacy and the passivity of reaction of early childhood. Flexibility—not rigidity—reflects an active self-direction. Furthermore, flexibility—not rigidity—reflects a genuinely objective attitude toward the world.

The fixed purposiveness of the rigid person narrows his interest in the world and restricts and prejudices his experience of it. He looks only for data—or, in the paranoid case, for clues —relevant to his purposes or concerns. The compulsive man who examines each woman with a checklist in mind of certain qualifications for marriage does not see that woman objectively; he sees a selection of traits and features whose sum is not a person but a high or a low score. This is a kind of subjectivity, an awareness that is not open and attentive to the world but is restricted and prejudiced by the necessity to satisfy pre-established requirements and fixed purposes. The volitional behavior of the rigid individual, in other words, is not guided by conscious aims and purposes that arise, as they normally do, out of objective attention to the world, out of a continuous judgment and a "trying on" in imagination of the possibilities of action. The rigid person's behavior is guided by fixed and already established purposes and is merely technically informed by data selected according to relevancy to those purposes. It is this process that results in the experience described by one compulsive man as living much of his life "on automatic pilot." It is the process involved in the behavior of rigid people as they plug away at their purposes mechanically and well beyond the point of their interest, in their routinized work, in their rituals, their recitation of dogma. Altogether, this volitional direction is far less autonomous than it appears to be. Strictly speaking, in many ways it is merely pseudo autonomous.

This pseudo autonomy is, I believe, an understandable outcome of the internal relationship with superior authority I have described. The aims and purposes that rigid individuals impose on themselves, and live under ("I should accomplish more." "I should move.") have precisely the character of established authoritative rules or imperatives. The rigid individual refers to these authoritative rules, as well as to actual models and images of authoritative figures, at exactly the point where the next person's attention and interest are directed to the external world. This is evident, for example, whenever an obsessive-compulsive person attempts to decide between x and y by referring to some rule, principle, or authoritative purpose or to what he imagines some respected figure would do—instead of simply looking at x and y. Or when he relies on authoritative dogma and is essentially uninterested in and inattentive to actual facts. Such decisions and judgments develop primarily out of the individual's relationship, not with the external world, but with certain internal representations of authority—that is, with an aspect of himself. To put the matter another way, the relationship of the rigid person to such authoritative rules and images substitutes for and makes unnecessary an objective relationship with the external world.

It is interesting to compare this process with the rigidity of young children whose behavior also is not guided by an objective relationship to the external world. Werner[1] describes, for example, the careful, plodding, often ceremonious way in which young children carry out familiar actions. Each step of the procedure must be properly executed, nothing must be left out, nothing hurried or compromised. It seems clear that the child has experienced the action, has recollected it, and therefore must reproduce it as a total sequential impression "which cannot be separated into the essential and the nonessential."[2] Werner adds, "In the last analysis . . . this rigidity and lack of plasticity in motive and

[1] Heinz Werner, *Comparative Psychology of Mental Development* (Chicago: Follett, 1948), pp. 206ff.
[2] Ibid., p. 207.

goal are grounded in the comparative lack of polarity between the subject and the world."[3] In other words, the child
has no clear and objective sense of the relation between
action and aim, and his action is not so much guided by
objective attention to the progress of the action and the
contingencies of external circumstance as it is triggered by
the aim and reeled off in a reactive sequence determined by
internal recollection.

The continued identification with superior authority and the
rigid will that is its product constitute an alternative to the
normal development of autonomy and ultimately constitute a
character with its own tendencies and dynamics. This identification is founded in the child's "unilateral respect" for the
superior authority of the adult, and, as I have suggested, it
preserves something of that relationship in its psychological
structure. Thus, while in normal development, that inequality
gradually diminishes, especially in adolescence, and is replaced
by self-respect and a sense of personal authority, the rigid
individual's self-respect remains invested in the achievements
of his will, in what he has "made of himself," and in his likeness
to those he actually regards as his betters. Such a self-respect
is easily distorted into pompousness, authoritarianism, or defensive pridefulness. There is a certain ironic inevitability in
the fact that those who feel small and most oppressively aware
and respectful of superior authority should for that reason
emulate that authority, base their self-respect on achieving a
likeness of it, and so, in a sense, continue to impose it on
themselves.

[3]Ibid., p. 211.

Chapter 4

Obsessive-Compulsive
Rigidity

I SHALL DESCRIBE here in more detail the nature of the compulsive person's rigidity, and I shall try to show its relation to certain of his characteristic attitudes, to subjective experience, to motivational experience, and also to certain specific traits and symptoms.

We know, for example, that compulsive people are typically characterized by extraordinary determination, tenacity, and stubbornness. Yet these strong, determined individuals may be thrown into a state of anxiety and confusion by what would be, to anyone else, a trivial decision. It is not difficult to see, at least in an abstract way, that these seemingly contradictory traits can be accounted for by the nature of rigidity. It is exactly in the nature of rigidity to be undeviating from an established course, yet incapable of initiating a new one. The problem remains, however, of understanding the attitudes, the kinds of conscious experience, and the volitional processes which comprise such rigidity in compulsive people and which account specifically for these traits.

Conscientiousness and the Experience of "I Should"

The rigidity of compulsive people actually consists of a special kind of conscientiousness. The compulsive person insists, for example, on doing the job "right"—that is, exactly according to established procedures or prescribed rules and regulations even when the rules do not quite apply; he insists on pursuing his purpose thoroughly, exhausting all possibilities long past the point of any reasonable chance of success; in general, he insists on doing the correct thing or sticking to the correct view, according to accepted principles or established practices, without regard for common sense, reasonable proportions, or particular circumstances. This is the most general meaning of compulsive rigidity. It is also the meaning—in the special case of matters of opinion—of dogmatism. Rigidity or dogmatism is behavior that is determined by prior internal requirements, requirements of duty, responsibility, or fidelity to authoritative rules, principles, or theories that make further judgment unnecessary. Indeed, from the standpoint of dogmatic attitudes, deviation from established principles—in other words, judgment—may be an act of weakness or even of impertinence.

It is well known that the compulsive person is in various ways extremely conscientious, that he tends to be concerned with moral evaluations and with doing the right thing where others may not see any moral issue at all, that he is typically hard-working, that his standards are fastidious, and so on. Yet all of this behavior is not in itself necessarily neurotic. Strong moral convictions, respect for high standards, devotion to work—these are not signs of rigid character or of any other kind of psychopathology. None of these characteristics nor all of them together are incompatible with autonomous judgment and flexible action. What makes the conscientiousness of the compulsive person special is different from the nature or the strength of his values, standards, and purposes. For all the intensity of his values, the compulsive person does not seem wholehearted about them; they do not seem thoroughly his own. His behavior does not follow from them spontaneously; on the contrary, he must constantly remind himself of them and nag himself about them. These are, in other words, not simply values, standards, and purposes but—something quite different—duties and responsibilities, values that the compulsive individual imposes on himself, values whose authority he regards as superior to his own values, inclinations, and judgments. They have, therefore, the status of rules and regulations. When the compulsive person, for example, reminds himself that he should do something because it is the right thing, the nice thing, or the generous thing, he is prompted not by kindness, generosity, or concern for justice but by a sense of rules and duty obliging him to do something kind, generous, or nice. This sense of duty is not altered by any actual disposition toward kindness or generosity. If he is inclined to give ten dollars, he will still think he should give fifteen.

His awareness of such duties and responsibilities is to one degree or another oppressive, and this oppressive tension gives rise to a special kind of motivation, the motivation to seek relief. This motivation therefore, unlike most motivations, does not reflect a relationship between the individual and the external world but reflects rather one between the individual and himself. Such a motivation prompts action that is not essentially responsive to the world's possibilities but is guided by prior internal requirements. This is dutiful action.

The most conspicuous subjective manifestation of this kind of conscientiousness, constantly experienced by compulsive people, is the imperative experience "I should." It is true that the nature of this imperative is not always explicit and by no means necessarily clear to the individual himself. He may say, "I must get the fence painted this weekend!" as though referring to some objective necessity, or, "I really want to read that book!" as though merely expressing a firm intention, as one would if determined to overcome some external obstacle. But there is no compelling objective necessity or external obstacle. The urgent tone typical of these declarations, their language of will and resolve—they invariably end as though with an exclamation mark—is directed at the speaker himself, at his own resistance or disinclination. That tone makes it clear that the meaning and experience of such declarations is the imperative "I should!" They are reminders of duty—directives, admonitions, or reproaches in the manner of a superior addressing a subordinate.

Thus, the imperative "I should" typically requires only a change of pronoun from first to second person to be identical to a parent's admonitions to a child, as when a young woman admonishes herself concerning a relationship she disapproves of: "I should stop seeing him! He's no good!" and so forth. At the same time, inasmuch as the speaker is the object of such admonitions, the experience of "I should" is oppressive.

The compulsive person lives in this way with a more or less continuous sense of duties and responsibilities, of rules, principles, standards, and images of various kinds concerning what he should do, what he should be, what he should be interested in, even what he should feel. These are not merely particular unwelcome duties or obligations prompted from time to time by circumstances. They are the general principles and standards that constitute a conscientious will, a mode of self-direction; and although they may be fully articulated only from time to time, they have more or less continuous application: one should take advantage of every opportunity; one should be mature and do the mature thing; one should never take the easy way out; and so on. It is not only that the compulsive person reminds himself continually of the duties that follow from such rules and principles; he also shrinks from action independent of these rules and principles. He regularly refers decisions and judgments to their authority—what would be the mature thing to do?—or to the standard of what some respected figure would do, think, or feel in such circumstances in order to determine what he should do, think, or feel. In other words, when other people look at the world's possibilities to make up their minds what they want to do next, the compulsive person consults himself, his rules, principles, models. Thus, the relationship with the external world which is normally contained in motivation and action is to some extent displaced by a relationship between the individual and himself. The autonomous relationship with the external world which is reflected in the normal motivational and volitional "I want to" is displaced by the dutiful "I should."

This is to say, also, that the compulsive individual is estranged from many of his actual motivations and feelings by his identification with what he thinks he should do, want, and feel. He imagines that he is interested in reading the educational book when he is actually interested only in *having* read it. In his determination to be mature, he imagines that he is mature when he is only stilted.

Work, Purpose, and Self-discipline

Above all, the conscientious person works hard. Uninterrupted work or, at any rate, some consciously purposeful activity is the hallmark of a dutiful existence. The accomplishment of one form or another of work is a constant preoccupation of the compulsive person. It is the principal exercise of his will and it is critical to his self-respect.

Compulsive people are constantly engaged in or at least concerned about producing or accomplishing. They are extraordinarily conscious of some aim or purpose beyond the activity itself, of its result. They value activity only by its result; only activity that can produce a result and can give the feeling of accomplishing is called "doing something."

It is not that these people are always occupied with work in the usual sense of job or project. Virtually all of life *becomes* work to them. Reading a book, listening to music are transformed into purposeful projects, projects of self-improvement, measured and valued accordingly. The living of life itself becomes work, like the running of a business, with mental records of its productiveness and of various kinds of successes, setbacks, and rates of progress. Often they feel under pressure of time and have deadlines in mind, such as the thirtieth birthday, for various achievements in career, financial status, and the like.

Thus, many occasions are experienced by the compulsive person in a special, double way. A nice weekend is also a successful accomplishment; a holiday spent alone is not merely lonely but wasted.

This kind of purposeful activity is not motivated simply by interest. It is dutiful activity. Its tense and driven style and, to some extent, the general nature of its purposes—for example, the emphasis on productiveness—reflect this fact. The compulsive person does not respect—often does not recognize—aims that are immediate, aims that follow from simple interest, activities that produce nothing beyond themselves or beyond his own satisfaction, especially his immediate satisfaction. Such activities—watching TV, reading a mystery story (unless for the larger purpose of relaxation), or even studying chemistry simply out of interest in chemistry (unless it "leads somewhere")—seem aim*less* to him. These activities seem "self-indulgent" and "a waste of time," "doing nothing." He counts living itself as wasted unless it "adds up to something."

In order to seem worthwhile, in other words, activities must achieve purposes that seem to the compulsive person superior to his interests, wishes, and personal satisfaction. His purposes must transcend mere personal interests and satisfaction. For this reason, in addition to the standard of productiveness, long-range goals are typically respected in principle over short-range ones, durable and cumulative results are favored over passing ones, the difficult and the not easily available is valued, again in principle, over the easily available, and so on. Whereas normally purposes reflect and serve the interests of the individual, for the compulsive person the relation is the other way around: he serves the superior requirements of the purpose. It is he who serves the cause of advancing his career. He must justify himself by his activity and work; he feels accountable for it; he measures himself by its results. In truth, he has more respect for his purposes and his accomplishments than for himself.

Many dutiful purposes, it is true, have their origins in genuine interests; and many of them, perhaps even a preponderance of them, continue to contain such interests. However such interests are not respected until they can be regarded as serving a higher purpose.

For example, some people must identify an educational purpose in reading a book before they feel comfortable enjoying it. One man, who obviously enjoyed travel would allow himself to take a trip only if he could arrange to do some business during it. Only in this way could he avoid feeling that his trip was frivolous and his time wasted.

The self-imposed regime of dutiful work and purpose is oppressive but, inasmuch as the compulsive person identifies with that regime and identifies its purposes as his own, he feels entitled by his work and accomplishments to self-respect and a sense of personal authority. He sees himself and respects himself in his role as worker and achiever, as doctor, writer, successful salesman—as productive and useful. Such conditional self-respect, however, is unreliable at best; the loss of a job, a failure—even succeeding at a rate that falls short of his expectations—may trigger depression and acute feelings of insufficiency.

In the absence of such failure, the compulsive person often harbors an exaggerated notion of the power of will and self-discipline, and he achieves an illusion of a kind of self-transcendence through them. He exaggerates the extent to which he has made himself what he is. He imagines that he can, and that he must, rise above himself by an effort of will, by his self-control, his accomplishments, and so on (he does not recognize the disrespect for what he is that is contained in his attitude) and that with sufficient self-discipline he can control, or should be able to control, even what he feels and wishes.

Thus, some compulsive people habitually speak of not "allowing" themselves to feel upset or disappointed or of not "giving in" to—not feeling—their feelings.

Such an exaggerated sense of will and self-transcendence is also unreliable. Occasions arise when such a person does feel upset, when he does not feel like working and cannot bring himself to, and the experience of such feelings—ordinary human feelings—may alarm him, trigger further concern that he is "being weak," or "losing his grip" on himself; and a circular reaction of disturbance and the alarmed sensation of disturbance may be set in motion.

Thus, the compulsive person's identification of himself with the regime of dutiful work and purpose transforms the subjective meaning of autonomy from being free to follow one's own wishes and live according to one's own lights to self-discipline, self-control, the subordination of one's wishes to one's will. Such a person lives, therefore, in a state of continuous tension between will and underlying inclination. Even innocuous interests (like watching television) may become antagonists of superior purpose and self-discipline and may be experienced as weakness or laziness. He may imagine that if he were to lose or relax his self-discipline or will power, to "give in" to himself, he would cease all worthwhile activity and become an idler, a "vegetable," an alcoholic, or worse. He does not recognize the possibility that worthwhile activity or achievment may come not only out of strong will but out of strong interest, as he does not recognize the possibility of self-respect based not on his achievment or his productiveness but on his existence.

Decision and Indecision

The disciplined and dutiful attitude, the rigid will, is not suited to making choices or decisions. No amount of will power or disciplined application will help one to make the simplest choice or decision, except for purely technical decisions. Disciplined, rigidly dutiful people are prepared to carry out decisions and to do so conscientiously, but they are not prepared to *make* decisions. And the more rigidly disciplined the individual— estranged as he is from his actual feelings and wishes—the less prepared he is to make a choice, and the more he will shrink from doing so.

The compulsive person may arrange his life to reduce the need for choices—he lives as much as possible by established routines—but choices are inescapable. Circumstances and opportunities arise that interrupt the routine and demand choices. Sometimes these involve conflicts between what one wants to do (whether he knows it or not) and what he thinks he should or should not do.

A young woman thinks she should not marry the man who has proposed to her—he fails to meet all sorts of objective qualifications: age, educational background, and so forth— although (it is clear to the observer, if not to her) she very much wants to marry him. She thinks she should say no to his proposal, but she cannot bring herself to; she wants to say yes, but she does not dare to.

But the most striking instances, and perhaps the most common, are when a choice must be made—often trivial in its consequences—that is simply outside the domain of "shoulds" and "should nots." Such questions as whether to go to the movies or what to order on the menu cannot easily be referred to established rules and moral principles, still less be settled by them. They are matters of taste or preference and conspicuously matters not of what one should do but of what one wants to do. It is on these occasions especially that the compulsive person may say in despair, "But I don't know what I want to do!"

The problem in all these cases is the same. It is not merely that the compulsive person is confronted with a circumstance for which, estranged from his own feelings, values, and wishes, he is unequipped. It is, rather, that he is confronted with a circumstance in which that estrangement is particularly difficult to maintain. His dutiful attitude cannot satisfy the requirements of the particular circumstance, and he is forced into a different attitude, into a more direct relationship with the world—forced to act on the basis of his own feelings and the strength of his own authority. To be more exact, he is not necessarily forced into a different attitude; he may only be forced to take special measures to avoid it.

In these circumstances, the compulsive person continues to search for an authoritative answer, an answer that will tell him what he *should* do; and he attempts to recast the problem into a form that will provide such an answer. Thus he may try to recast a problem of personal choice into an objective, technical problem, with an objective, correct solution. He tries to add up pros and cons of unquantifiable matters, such as whether to marry a certain person, in the hope of arriving at an objective, and therefore authoritative, answer. He tries to find a general rule or higher purpose on the basis of which he can construe one or another alternative as the right thing to do. He is grateful if the problem of what to choose from the menu can be decided on the basis of health or economy; or if the problem of whether to go to the concert can be decided according to the rule that one should not miss a unique opportunity.

Sometimes a compulsive person, especially one who is a patient in psychotherapy, devises the rule that one *should* do what one "really" wants to do. He may try to find out what he "really" wants to do by self-examination. (The normal person, however, discovers what he wants to do not by looking inside himself but by looking outside at actual opportunities.)

Such efforts to find what he "really" wants to do are frequently unavailing; and the more conscientious the individual, the more likely they are to be so. He can find no convincing principle or objective solution, or he discovers half-convincing ones on both sides. When—despite his efforts to determine in an objective and authoritative way what he "really" wants to do—a compulsive person experiences himself actually leaning toward action one way or the other, in the absence of an authoritative direction, he is likely to feel anxious. He may shrink then from the incipient decision, challenge its authority, and subject it to the most searching and conscientious review: "Is it the right thing to do?" "Should I?" "Do I really want to?" This anxious critical review, prompted by the experience of choosing, may result in a reversal, a leaning in the alternative direction, in turn prompting a repetition of the process, a critical review from the alternative, original standpoint. He cannot find a satisfactory rule, but he cannot escape from his conscientiousness either. He cannot, for example, take the decision more lightly; its objective consequences may be trivial, but the attitude of simple personal choice feels bold. This tortured scrupulosity at the moment of choice is called "obsessional indecision."

Worry, Obsessional Thoughts, and Ritual

There is no doubt that the driven, purposeful activity and work of compulsive people accomplishes a great deal that is objectively valuable. Sometimes, of course, the product may suffer from rigidity or excessive conscientiousness—too much editing scratches the movie film—but it is at least as likely that the quality of the product will benefit. There are, however, certain kinds of compulsive activity, work of a sort, that have no objective product at all. Obsessional worry and other obsessional thinking have no objective results; compulsive ritual has objective results, but without productive value. Yet all of these are dutiful or conscientious activities and are motivated and shaped by processes and attitudes similar to those that are responsible for compulsive activity in general.

To a conscientious person, the existence of a problem, an uncertainty, a hazard, or a mistake imposes the responsibility to do something about it. The awareness of something being wrong, not as it should be, or not taken care of, in other words, imposes the responsibility to take corrective or precautionary action. To a person of exceptional dutifulness, even a possibility of something of this sort, perhaps even the barest possibility, imposes such responsibility. He conscientiously pursues any hint of problem or trouble, always concerned more about paying it too little attention than too much. When the possibilities of trouble are small, he pursues those small possibilities, and within those possibilities he discerns still further possibilities. Every physical symptom might be cancer or heart attack, every drop in business might be the beginning of the end, every school examination might be failure, and every failed examination might have disastrous consequences. In short, he assumes the worst.

Yet the person who worries in this way, obsessively, does not necessarily take corrective or precautionary action, at least not in the ordinary sense. It is true that he may be concerned with matters, such as a recent examination, where no action, or no further action, is possible. But even where action is perfectly feasible, it is not the rule. The man who worries obsessively about cancer is by no means sure to go to the doctor; the woman who worries about losing her job ("They'll fire me! I know it!") is not necessarily ready to start looking for another job. The impetus to act, in these cases, does not match the apparent intensity of concern. In other words, the concern is somewhat forced, worked up, and the worrier is not genuinely convinced of the necessity for action. He does not completely believe in the disasters that he worries about. If he did, he would behave differently.

He does not completely believe in the likelihood of disaster; but as a person of special conscientiousness he cannot dismiss or take the possibility lightly either. He feels that he *should* take such possibilities seriously, should regard them with sufficient concern or alarm, should assume the worst. Any other attitude seems to him irresponsible and careless, inviting trouble by its nonchalance, or—as one such person put it—"living in a fool's paradise." Hence the exaggerated concern of such worries and the emphatic, forced style with which they are typically pronounced ("They'll fire me!" or "I failed!" or "It's probably cancer!"). They are pseudo actions, ritualistic substitutes for actual precautions against disaster; the worrier has constantly to remind himself of the possibility of such disaster and pay it respectful and concerned attention.

Since such worry is essentially forced and obligatory and reflects neither genuine judgment of circumstances nor the actual level of concern about them, it is formalistic or ritualistic in quality: it is, for example, repetitious.

A man discovers a sore in his mouth and declares to his wife, "It's probably malignant! What do you think?" She reminds him that on previous occasions such sores have turned out to have no medical significance, and he feels better. A half-hour later he turns to her again, "Still it might be cancer! Do you think so?" He repeats this many times, forgets, remembers, and takes it up again in the same words.

If this understanding is correct, obsessive worrying, no less than compulsive work and purposeful activity in general, is a manifestation of the rigid, dutiful, compulsive will. It seems strange, I realize, to regard worry as willful, even rigidly dutiful. The person who worries obsessively is certainly more likely, to the extent that he is aware of the tendency, to regard his worry as an affliction that, far from being willful, occurs against his will and despite his wish to relax. As a tendency, of course, it certainly is an affliction and a reflection of a psychological makeup that is, indeed, of no one's choice or making. But it is precisely the nature of that affliction that the compulsive individual cannot neglect to think on any possibility of trouble or disaster without an intolerable feeling of irresponsibility and recklessness. There is no doubt either that worrying can be exceedingly oppressive, just as the constant burden of any duty can be. But the oppressive experience of worry, like the strain and tension of compulsively driven work, is itself an effect of a dutiful and coercive will exercised here in the forcing of oneself, again and again, to imagine the worst, not to shrink from it, to exhaust all its possibilities. It may be said, in fact, that for some people worrying can be as driven and obligatory as work is for others.

In one important matter that directly affects one's subjective experience of it, worry is different from even relentlessly driven work. In the case of work, the compulsive individual's conscientious harassment and coercion of himself is ultimately aimed at, and is to some extent relieved by, productive activity. Furthermore, the burdensome responsibility to accomplish the work is usually diluted to greater or lesser extent by his genuine interest in it or in its accomplishment. In the case of worry, on the other hand, the aim and the final result of such coercion is actually to impose a distressed state of mind on the worrier himself.

Another compulsive (or obsessional) experience closely related to worrying, although less common, is the obsessive thought—such as the thought, when in a high place, of impulsively jumping off—which is extremely discomforting and sometimes horrifying. Such thoughts are not merely recurrent, often being triggered regularly by certain commonplace circumstances, but once triggered, they cannot be dismissed and must constantly be returned to. They may include, for example, thoughts of losing control and committing violent and abhorrent acts against oneself, like the one I mentioned, or jumping in front of a train or cutting off one's penis; or acts against others, especially someone else who is loved and innocent, such as a child. Or they may be thoughts of impulsively committing less horrifying but still extremely improper or shocking acts, such as shouting obscenities, vomiting, or making vulgar sexual advances. There are many other much more common though less dramatic kinds of obsessive thoughts as well, including bitterly regretful recollections of certain past events, especially mistakes ("Maybe I shouldn't have . . ."), or thoughts of contracting some dreadful disease. Some of these obsessions are much like common worries, except that they are more isolated and fixed, sometimes persisting in the same form over many years.

As far as their content is concerned, all these thoughts are extremely unpleasant, uncomfortable, or dreadful; and this discomfort makes their evidently compelling interest difficult to understand. One can hardly escape the impression, in fact, that it is their discomfort that makes them so compelling. This notion receives a certain confirmation in some obsessional thoughts about impulsive acts. These obsessions may include the idea that the impulsive act—jumping off the balcony, for instance—may actually be induced or triggered by the thought itself; and this very idea seems to drive the obsessive person to a still further pursuit of the thought, as if he were driven to test the safety of the ice.

The ambiguity or, rather, the duality of subjective experience which is characteristic of compulsive activity in general is especially striking in the case of obsessive thoughts. On the one hand, the individual feels as though these thoughts are forced upon him and he cannot expel them from his mind: the experience seems to him not merely involuntary and unwelcome but actually coercive. On the other hand, it seems clear that once even a fragment of the thought comes to mind, he forces himself to play it out completely, even exhaustively; he presses it to its limits. The process can only be described by saying that the individual feels *obliged* to force himself through it. This, of course, is exactly the experience, in a particularly acute form, of a rigidly dutiful attitude and will.

This process is striking, for example, in the case of obsessional regrets. For the obsessional man even the most peripheral reminder of the woman he thinks he (possibly) should have married—a name, a date—is enough to prompt him to a review of what he did wrong, its ruinous consequences, how it might have been, and so on. Such a review is conducted with an excruciating conscientiousness: the obsessional person leans over backward to make sure that he does not underestimate the consequences of his mistake, that he does not, in other words, let himself off too lightly. Hence, the mistake is exaggerated— it is always irretrievable and grave; the opportunity, lost perhaps many years before, is always once-in-a-lifetime.

The thoughts a person has reflect his interests—not only his wishes or motivations but also his anxieties or concerns. He may not be aware of those interests or concerns, but they will be reflected in the thoughts that circumstances, even incidental circumstances, bring to his mind. The obsessively conscientious person is constantly concerned about what he should not do or should not have done, should not feel or think. In this sense, the thought of the impermissible in one form or another and the exaggerated specter of its consequences is never far from his mind. Obsessive thoughts of "losing control" and doing shocking, violent, dangerous things are such specters, just as the thought of the ruinous mistake is. They are, just as all obsessive worries are, the exaggerated specters created by an obsessive conscientiousness.

Such a specter may appear first at a time of special worry or guilty concern. A middle-aged, recently divorced woman became obsessed with the "impulse to vomit" and the thought that she might "lose control" and vomit at any time. This obsession developed after some sexual experiences and the worry that she might become "promiscuous."

Sometimes one such obsessive specter leads to further ones. For example, a tense, worried young man, a student from an underdeveloped country, became obsessed with the thought that he might catch a repulsive skin disease after meeting a person who had such a condition. As the obsessive thought continued, he became alarmed that he was having such "crazy ideas" and then became obsessed with the thought that he would "go crazy," return home in disgrace, and so on.

In many obsessive individuals, the mere reminder of a mistake automatically prompts the renewal of obsessive regret, or the mere presence of a situation that, without caution, might be dangerous—standing on a subway platform, for example—regularly triggers the specter of "losing control" and jumping off.

Once such a specter appears, it becomes the object of obligatory concern. When reminded of it, one must re-imagine it and create it anew. This process is called obsession.

Worried, obsessive thought and the exhaustive pursuit of the worst possibilities, are often exceedingly uncomfortable, but to the rigid, dutiful person, the alternative is intolerable. Painful, even agonizing, as the conscientious attitude may be, it is his attitude; from his standpoint, to fail to be concerned about losing self-control is to abandon self-control, not to be concerned about what one might have done wrong is to do wrong, to neglect any possible source of concern—not to lean over backward to worry over and think about what, perhaps, *should* be worried over and thought about—can only feel incautious or irresponsible. Hence, he finds specters that even to him become far-fetched.

Compulsive ritual may be so conspicuously odd and strike the observer as so pointless that its relationship to the general tendency of rigid but productive compulsive activity can easily be overlooked. The fact is that all rigid, dutiful behavior becomes ritualistic after a certain point. To the extent that any action is carried out simply for the sake of satisfying the prior requirements of rules or the prescriptions of duty (such as prescriptions of generosity, propriety, completeness, or cleanliness), it tends not only to be rigid but also ritualistic. It tends, in other words, to satisfy these formal requirements in merely formal, technical, or ceremonial ways. It is apparent, in fact, that the most ordinary sort of rigid, dutiful behavior—the somewhat artificial niceness of some compulsive people, their solicitousness, their propriety, certainly their orderliness—tends to be ceremonial and ritualistic.

Ritual action is fundamentally different from regular action. It lacks what might easily be considered the essential significance of action—the aim of effecting some objective change. It is not aimed at altering the relationship of the individual to his environment in some more satisfactory way. It is aimed at altering the individual's relationship with himself, at achieving peace of mind, merely by the performance of the act itself. If there are any objective effects of the action—moving a spoon from this place to that, cleaning of the hands, and so on—they merely signify that the required action has been carried out; in themselves they have no importance whatever.

Compulsive ritual, therefore, is rigid, dutiful action of an extreme sort, in which purely formal requirements of duty have entirely replaced interest in external goals. This fact has two consequences: ritual is more acutely obligatory than dutiful action ordinarily is—the individual feels "compelled" to perform it—while at the same time ritual lacks the usual reasons for action, and thus seems meaningless to the observer. The nature of these obligatory activities is consistent with the general nature of compulsive duties and responsibilities: rituals consist on the whole of exaggeratedly conscientious corrective and precautionary measures, such as might be required against some possibility, typically a remote or purely technical possibility, of mishap. Ritual typically consists, in other words, of special, exaggeratedly conscientious, corrective or precautionary procedures which are prompted by special, exaggeratedly conscientious concerns. Thus, it may consist of further dutiful or responsible procedures prompted by the compulsive person's concern that he has not carried out his regular responsibilities or duties with proper thoroughness—as when he repeats several times turning the gas stove on, then off. The style of ritual —exaggerated care, preciseness, repetition—is consistent with its conscientious purposes. Checking the gas stove a certain number of times, arranging then rearranging eating utensils and plates in a precise sequence of steps—these actions reflect an attitude of responsible concern carried to extraordinary lengths.

To say that such precautions and corrections are exaggeratedly conscientious, or that they are experienced as obligatory, is to say that their interest is not *actually* precautionary or corrective, but that they are merely dutiful *ceremonies* of precaution or correction. They are, in other words, not motivated by anxiety about objective mishap. On the contrary, both the specter of the possibility of mishap and the ritualistic precautionary or corrective action are products of an exhaustive, obsessive, conscientiousness which first raises a specter and then demands action against it. The ritualistic precaution or correction, therefore, is an extension of the obsessive concern and may be followed by further obsessive concerns. In this way, elaborate rituals can be constructed out of a succession of obsessive concerns and dutiful precautions or corrections. Each dutiful action is itself subject to further review and concern; each correction is conscientiously challenged and subject to further correction; each precaution scrupulously examined for insufficiencies requiring further precaution. The hands that have just been washed have now, in the act of turning off the water, touched the spigot, raising again the possibility of contamination and the necessity for further procedures. As with compulsive activity in general, these concerns and procedures are driven by a conscientiousness that will not be lastingly satisfied, a conscientiousness that forbids any final satisfaction of its requirements, any lasting sense of relief or contentment.

In this way obsessive concern can become increasingly technical and precautionary, or corrective procedures can become increasingly complicated or can threaten to become so. These procedures may be finally subject to further technical revision for the sake of economy and condensed into a prescribed sequence of token acts. Thus, rituals frequently involve doing something a prescribed number of times, obviating the threat of an indefinite progression of complications.

One woman had a nightly prayer ritual that she ended by asking God's blessing on an increasing number of individuals, then groups of individuals. Still concerned lest she omit someone who should be included, she hit upon the economical device of asking for a blessing for all those who deserved it, and thus shifted the responsibility to God.

Some compulsive rituals, especially those, I believe, that are well established, are carried out purely as obligatory acts without consciousness of specific precautionary or corrective concerns apart from concerns with the proper execution of the ritual itself. The compulsive person may execute the ritual, in other words, somewhat as a dutiful technician, military officer, or religious worshiper might carry out obligatory tasks—with great care but with neither knowledge of nor interest in their further purpose or significance. The compulsive ritual, it is true, feels more coercive, especially if it becomes time-consuming and troublesome, since it lacks even a semblance of objective purpose. Even so, such ritual reflects, with the clarity of an extreme case, the general nature of a dutiful attitude and the rigid behavior that follows from it. It is not so different from the attitude of the military officer, for whom rules and regulations are to be obeyed, not questioned, or that of the orthodox religious worshiper for whom any slight deviation he might make from prescribed procedures is in principle an impermissible substitution of his authority for the Church's.

Chapter 5

Sadism and Masochism: General Tendencies

Sadism and masochism have come to refer both to sexual interest and satisfaction in cruelty, especially in cruel domination and submission, and to general tendencies, particularly those in personal relations. The subject of this and the following chapter, which specifically concerns sexual sadism and masochism, is the psychology of certain interests in cruelty, from the standpoints of both the one—in our society primarily the man—who inflicts suffering on others and the one—primarily the woman—who seems to inflict it on herself or, at least, to endure it habitually and by choice.

How is this subject related to rigid character and the problem of autonomy? Let me only suggest at this point that cruelty of this sort involves coercive relationships or relationships between superior and inferior—the degradation or humiliation of one by another; the imposing of will by one, the surrender of the other—or, at least, fantasies of such relationships. Concern with such relationships is to some extent common to all rigid characters.

In psychoanalysis there has long been established a clinical association between sadism and various traits and symptoms of rigid character—or, rather, of anal character—particularly certain compulsive traits and obsessional symptoms.[1] The clinical association gave rise to the conception of a specifically anal sadistic stage of development, referring to the aggressive (sadistic) potentialities and impulses inherent in the development of bowel control and the period of intensified anal eroticism. The conception offered an explanation for certain compulsive or obsessional traits or symptoms as reaction formations against sadistic impulses, as well as for compulsive conscientiousness in general. Furthermore, in the assertive willfulness of sadism or its assertion of power through the degradation of its victim, it is not at all difficult to see modes and aims that may have sources in the impulses of an anal sadistic stage. Nevertheless, the fact remains that identification of a contemporary condition with a historical source—or, specifically, identification of a pathology of autonomy with certain of its rudimentary forerunners—simplifies and distorts its picture. This is simply too narrow a base from which to derive the complicated aims and forms of sadism, even less of masochism. Neither can be reduced to, or accounted for by, such impulses; such behavior is the product of a frame of mind.

---

[1] See Sigmund Freud, "The Predisposition to Obsessional Neurosis (1913)," Collected Papers, vol. II (London: Hogarth Press and Institute of Psychoanalysis, 1949), pp. 122–32.

Sadism

The aims of sadism are, as I said, not only to make the victim suffer but especially to humiliate or degrade him, to make him feel helpless or powerless, to "put him in his place" or "show him who's boss." In the mildest case, the sadist wishes to make his victim feel ridiculous and small; in the most extreme case, to abuse him in such a way as to destroy his self-respect, break his will, make him give in. These are aggressive aims of a special kind—not at all like destructiveness, for example, as Fromm points out.[2] To Fromm (who revises the Freudian conception of anal character to what he calls the "hoarding character," and severs its dependence on instinctual development), the essence of these aims, the essence of sadism, is "the passion to have absolute and unrestricted control over a living being."[3] The experience of such control is an experience of power; it transforms, he says, "impotence into the experience of omnipotence."[4] This psychological orientation, Fromm says, is also manifest as the "authoritarian character," an individual who respects power and the powerful above all and despises weakness and helplessness, who tyrannizes those beneath him and is submissive to, wishes to "fuse" with, the powerful ones above.[5]

This view accounts for many aspects of sadism: for example, the important fact that the sadistic person regularly chooses his victims from those who are subordinate to him, the comparatively powerless, those he can control. It is, in fact, entirely plausible that such an interest in control or "discipline" of

[2]Erich Fromm, *The Anatomy of Human Destructiveness* (New York: Fawcett, 1973).
[3]Ibid., pp. 322ff.
[4]Ibid., p. 323.
[5]Erich Fromm, *Escape from Freedom* (New York: Rinehart, 1941).

another person is in some way an extension of the rigid character's interest in self-control and self-discipline, and that it reinforces his sense of personal authority, strength, and will. Anyone who has dealt with a rigid person knows very well that his unbending and disciplined purposiveness frequently forces those around him to bend. It may be said that the point at which such a *willingness* to make others bend becomes an *interest* in making others bend marks the transition from stubbornness to sadism, and clinical experience teaches us that this is an easy and familiar transition. Yet there are important distinctions between the two attitudes, and these distinctions are blurred when one attempts to encompass them both in a single mode. There are aspects of sadism, of cruelty, that, it seems to me, cannot plausibly be explained by any degree of interest in mere control of another individual. An aggressive satisfaction—a satisfaction in the other's suffering as such, perhaps even a hatred—is an essential and undeniable part of sadism.

I have already referred to the fact that the target of the sadistic person is the subordinate, the comparatively powerless one, the one he regards as weak or inferior. Sadism is to be found in the sergeant's behavior toward recruits, in the boss's toward his employees, in the husband's toward his wife, in the adult's toward the child. Even in certain apparent exceptions, such as the sadistic cruelties that children may perpetrate on a teacher, the victim will be that teacher who seems relatively powerless and weaker than the others. It is not simply a question of the safety or the feasibility of such targets; these are the individuals who excite sadistic interest. To put the matter another way, to inflict suffering on a relatively powerless individual, an "inferior," or to inflict further suffering on one who is already suffering, is the intrinsic nature of sadism. Aggression as an assault on one who is capable of defense, is, as Fromm points out,[6] a different experience and reflects a different interest. The attitude from which sadism emerges is the contemptuous attitude of the superior toward the inferior. Indeed, sadism is a special expression of this contempt.

It is not difficult to understand the existence of such attitudes and relationships in light of the psychology of rigid character. These individuals continually take their own measure, and many rigid persons live with a self-important consciousness of their superior achievements, rank, and authority, their membership in some prestigious group or category. This kind of consciousness of one's quality and concern with measures of it always contains a consciousness of the comparative quality of others, an awareness of superior figures and of lesser ones, of those inferior in position or achievement, for example, and therefore inferior in quality. An exorbitant respect for some people implies a corresponding disdain for others. Sometimes this disdain takes comparatively benign, or at least comparatively inconspicuous forms, as in the patronizing attitude that many "strong" men of this psychological makeup have toward women.

At the same time, beyond the mere consciousness of superior and inferior, the rigid character who is in a position of some actual authority is sometimes a martinet. His sense of personal authority is exaggerated and self-conscious; hence he is authoritarian, dogmatic. His standards and the general tendency of his attitudes are likely to be conservative and proper, since they draw heavily on his respect for established authority. These individuals believe that such respect for authority, discipline, obedience, and perhaps even coercion and what others may see as cruelty, are necessary and valuable in the relations between superior and subordinate, parent and child, teacher and stu-

[6]Fromm, *Human Destructiveness* [2], p. 325.

dent. They are necessary for proper training, the maintenance of order and proper standards, the development of character,[7] the fulfillment of responsibilities.

All this is not necessarily sadism, but it has a certain kinship to sadism. We know that sadism is regularly associated with and justified by pedagogical, moral, disciplinary, or corrective purposes, that sadistic behavior is often supposed to teach the child, the prisoner, the subordinate, the recruit respect for authority and "right" values and standards. This association is no accident. Sadism is associated with such purposes and can easily be wrapped in them because it is a product of the same frame of mind that gives rise to them, or at least is a product of that frame of mind under certain special conditions of tension.

When his already exaggerated and uncertain sense of personal authority is chafed further by feelings of inferiority, shame, and humiliation, the rigid individual may become defensive, his attitudes harder and angrier. He becomes acutely conscious of his own and others' relative rank and quality; he becomes more rigidly authoritarian, sometimes haughty or arrogant, and more punitive; and his attitude toward subordinates or those he regards as inferior, weak, or lacking in discipline becomes actively contemptuous.[8] Such persons—who, for certain rigid men, may include women in general and, even more, "effeminate" men—embody what the rigid individual is ashamed of, defensively repudiates, and therefore hates. He regards them as unworthy of respect. He is disgusted by them,

[7] An extreme example of these views is the case of Dr. Schreber, nineteenth-century authority on child rearing and father of the paranoid schizophrenic Daniel Paul Schreber, subject of Freud's study of paranoia (see chapter 7).

[8] In Fromm's discussion of Heinrich Himmler's sadism, there is an ironic example of this haughty contempt in the attitude of the German general, Heinz Guderian, *toward* Himmler: "This insignificant man, with all signs of racial inferiority . . ." (*Human Destructiveness* [2], p. 335).

sometimes outraged by them, even obsessively so; and if he is also in a position of actual power or authority, he may be driven to punish them. This contemptuous punishment of weakness or inferiority, especially unrepentant inferiority, of the undisciplined, the disrespectful, is what we call sadism.[9]

Such punishment is far more aggressive, far angrier, than seems implied by Fromm's conception of an urge for absolute control, but it is much more specific in both aims and form than mere "aggression" suggests. Its form reflects its essential nature: to punish "weakness" by "discipline," to shame inferiority and make it aware of itself by humiliation and degradation, to "show who's boss," to "teach a lesson" in respect for authority by forcing surrender to authority—all sometimes mixed with an actual interest in the victim's edification, sometimes rationalized by such interest, sometimes with the conscious, angry sense that the victim deserves it.

Military organization is intrinsically authoritarian so it is not surprising to find there unusually clear examples of the nature of sadism. I refer, for instance, to the sadistic practices of Marine Corps boot camp (probably much the same practices, in moderate degree, characterize military recruit training in general).[10] Boot camp recruits are treated with systematic and explicit contempt (largely by noncommissioned officers); they are subjected to a barrage of insults and humiliations, disciplinary coercion, intimidation, and demands for absolute obedience—all directed at and obviously punishing their presumed civilian weakness of character, lack of discipline, unmanliness.

[9]The idea of punishing inferiority, or that weakness may be punished as an offense, is not strange from the point of view of authoritarian discipline, which does not sharply distinguish weakness and inferiority (not being what one should be) from disobedience, disorderliness, or impropriety (being what one should not be): both reflect lack of discipline.

[10]See H. Paul Jeffers and Dick Levitan, *See Parris and Die: Brutality in the U.S. Marines* (New York: Hawthorn Books, 1971).

The physical demands made on them are so extreme as to be clearly beyond the requirements of physical conditioning and actually constitute further humiliating punishment of physical weakness and inferiority. It is difficult to separate the purely sadistic aim of punishment ("discipline") of the recruits' undisciplined civilian mentality from an interest in actually instilling military discipline; that is, it is difficult to separate the interest in "teaching them a lesson" from the interest in actually teaching them a lesson. The military point of view assumes that the instilling of military as well as personal discipline in place of undisciplined civilian independence or "weakness" requires coercive authority and punishment. It may well be that this view is correct, and that these methods are successful, according to their aims.

There is a further effect of this training process. The achievement of success in the form not only of respect for military authority but also of an identification with that respected authority, creates a new generation of authoritarianism and even sadism, at least temporarily. Successful recruits commonly develop a contempt not merely toward the enemy (which was officially encouraged in the Vietnam War[11]) but —more striking—toward unsuccessful, perhaps incorrigibly civilian, or "weak" recruits.

A recruit says, "It's hard, but I like it. They're strict. The Marine Corps is hard on discipline. If you can take the orders, sir, you can make it in the Marine Corps, sir. In our platoon there's only a few that don't give a damn. Sooner or later they'll get rid of them and we'll have a damn good platoon."[12] There is no doubt that "weaker" recruits frequently become the ob-

[11]Chaim F. Shatan, "The Subversion of the Super-ego: Uses of Identification with the Aggressor in Basic Combat Training," unpublished manuscript, 1972.
[12]Jeffers and Levitan, *See Parris and Die* [10], pp. 74–75.

jects of contemptuous sadistic punishment at the hands of successful, newly strong, and disciplined recruits.

Masochism

Does the masochistic person actually look for pain and inflict it on himself? Does he find satisfaction in pain, humiliation, defeat, and suffering as he is supposed to according to popular conception? Masochism is a peculiar notion and has always been troublesome in psychiatry: both its motives and the nature of its satisfaction have been unclear. This unclarity has no doubt been responsible for the somewhat indiscriminate use of the term in psychiatry. For example, suffering that may merely be *tolerated* as an acceptable price to pay for other satisfactions, as in a complicated love affair, is sometimes assumed to be masochistically *satisfying*.

The case of sexual masochism is in certain ways less ambiguous. For some people the idea of suffering physical torture, coercion, and humiliation is highly erotic. The explanation of this sexual interest is a problem itself, but its nature at least is clear. As for the other behavior that we call masochistic, however, even its satisfactions, the conscious feelings that prompt it, the attitudes that surround it, are all in doubt.

There is no doubt, though, about its existence. I am referring not only to self-inflicted physical pain that is not evidently erotic but, more common, various sorts of exaggerated self-depreciation and demeaning humility and deference and also —probably the most common form of masochism—the chronic, usually bitter exaggeration and "nursing" of humiliations, defeats, and injustices. These instances of self-inflicted suffering are authentic phenomena of masochism. To understand them, it is not enough to speak of unconscious motivations or impulses. They also involve conscious aims and interests, feelings, attitudes—once again, a frame of mind. The problem is to understand the frame of mind to which this strange, paradoxical behavior is satisfying or, at least, necessary.

The following incident was related by a thirty-six-year-old woman. It offers an example of a certain kind of masochistic satisfaction. It involves self-inflicted discomfort and the "nursing" and exaggeration of an injustice.

She had been returning from a shopping expedition with her husband and baby the day before. In the bus station she had quarreled with her husband over who was to carry which of their numerous packages and bundles. She, already burdened with the baby stroller, had asked her husband to take some of the packages she was carrying; but he, already carrying a number of his own, had refused. They came to a flight of stairs. At this point it was obvious that she could not manage both her packages and the stroller without great difficulty, and her husband moved to take the stroller or some of her packages. She, however, glared at him coldly and proceeded to struggle up the stairs with all her packages and the stroller, ignoring his repeated requests to be permitted to relieve her. Without any help, she made it to the top. By this time, she could tell, her husband was quite upset. She, on the other hand, obviously experienced a satisfaction that, in fact, returned to her face as she reached this point in telling the story. Nevertheless she asked, now somewhat irritated with herself, why did she go through all this difficulty? why didn't she accept her husband's offer when it finally was made?

One can easily answer these questions. It is true that she seized an opportunity to suffer and refused to relinquish it; but in doing so, she achieved not merely a satisfaction but actually a kind of triumph. She achieved what is called a "moral victory."

It is interesting to examine this particular moral victory more closely, to see exactly what it consisted of and especially how it was achieved. This woman had just experienced a defeat at the hands of superior forces; her husband refused to help her, and she could do nothing about it. She was, as it happens, a rather prideful person, a person of sensitive dignity, who took such defeats hard, easily feeling humiliated by them. There is no doubt that she initially felt so in this case. By behaving as she did, however, she was able to transcend her initial powerlessness and humiliation. By refusing to allow her husband to retreat from the consequences of his attitude, and by seizing the opportunity to increase and underscore the burdens he had imposed, she exposed his inconsiderateness and demonstrated her own strength, dignity, and moral superiority. By deliberately inflicting on herself an exaggerated and demonstrative form of what he originally inflicted on her, she transformed her position from a powerless and subjugated one to a strong and dignified one. She took charge of the action and transformed its significance in the only way it was possible for her to do so —much as a boatman, caught in a powerful current he cannot oppose, maintains control of his boat by rowing in the direction of the current but faster than it.

On the other hand, acceptance of her husband's belated offer to help—an offer of a truce, of an end to hostilities— would have allowed her initial defeat and humiliation to stand, allowed him to get away with it. It would have been, from her standpoint, an act of resignation, a giving-in. It would have been an act of weakness in a further sense—a giving-in to herself—for it would have sacrificed dignity and principle to physical comfort and convenience. In this connection, masochism is often considered to be a passive, acquiescent mode of behavior—as willingness to accept suffering or abuse may easily appear to be. On the contrary, willingness to accept suffering in order to make a point, to uphold a principle, or to maintain self-respect, reflects great determination and will.

Moral victories like this one are satisfying, but they are not always to be had. The more powerful aggressor may be indifferent to the injustice done to his victim, for example, or he may be gone from the scene. It is true that the victim can even so achieve a sense of moral superiority, but that is not the same as a victory. In any case, the principle of moral victory is too narrow to encompass all of masochistic behavior. It is a special case, although an important one. It may be, in fact, that the whole picture of masochistic satisfaction has been overdrawn. After all, people—especially neurotic people—sometimes behave as they do not so much to achieve gains as to forestall further losses; and much masochistic behavior seems to be aimed less at achieving victory over superior forces than at mitigating the experience of helpless and humiliating defeat.

I am referring particularly to those individuals who are chronically aggrieved, constantly preoccupied with their sufferings. These people complain a great deal about having been victimized or unfairly treated, and they seem to exaggerate their troubles—for example, by constant and melodramatic reference to their "hurt" or "pain." This behavior gives the complainer a bad reputation among his friends, who come to suspect that he is prolonging his suffering, indulging in exhibitionism or making excessive demands for sympathy and attention. Such suspicions are not altogether justified. Masochistic people share the general human need for sympathy and recognition, but they dwell upon and exaggerate their misfortunes not merely, nor even primarily, for an external audience. They exaggerate their sufferings to themselves. To put it simply, they seem to work themselves up, to try to experience more suffering than they actually feel at the time. Hence, their suffering seems forced, their look of suffering artificial, their language melodramatic. Even their voices are sometimes strained and nasal in the way that is called "whiny." The masochistic person seems to take note of his actual suffering when it does occur —to mark it down, as it were, as though to be sure that it does not pass unnoticed—and to remind himself at certain times that suffering is warranted. Thus, when an old misfortune comes to mind in an incidental or peripheral way, or when an old grievance threatens to grow faint, he tries to retrieve it and to revive the experience of it. He cannot allow the grievance to dissipate or himself to forget it. In short, he is obsessed with his misfortunes.

For example, a woman of forty-four, who had been left by her husband several years earlier, was "reminded" constantly and sometimes by the most oblique connections (meeting an acquaintance, a holiday, an anniversary of the occasion when they did this or that) of him, their relationship, and her "hurt." She was often prompted by these associations to review not only this episode but also a series of other injustices in her earlier life and childhood—old rebuffs, childhood defeats, and so on—and spoke melodramatically of the "pain," "hurt," or psychological damage involved in them, of how easily she had been exploited or victimized, and so on.

Why should someone repeatedly, obsessively, remind herself of, exaggerate, "nurse," old defeats and injustices that have obviously hurt her and wounded her pride? The problem has variations. Another form appears in certain cases of obsessive jealousy. The jealous person feels victimized and humiliated on account of some past unfaithfulness of a lover. Every reminder of that unfaithfulness revives and intensifies his bitterness; yet he insists on hearing all the details of those humiliating events again and again. He may refer to them for years afterward, refusing to allow them to fade or be forgotten, continuing to work up old feelings about them. It is true that the jealousy of the masochistic person, in reviving old defeats or humiliations, usually makes or implies a moral charge; but he shows little evidence in these instances of a sense of moral victory and none at all of the martyr's serenity. On the contrary, what is much in evidence is bitterness and grudge, an aggravated, rankling sense of continuing, unrectified injustice. That is just the point, however: if the masochistic person has not achieved a moral victory, he is not willing to accept defeat either.

Masochistic people are frequently urged by their friends to do just that, to forget old grievances and let bygones be bygones; but the significance of keeping those grievances alive can be judged from their reactions to such suggestions. They feel, as I suggested earlier, that to forget an injustice or a humiliation is to allow it to stand unrectified, to accept it, to "give in," to take the easy way out, to abandon protest and, therefore, altogether to abandon one's rights and self-respect. It would be, as one such person put it, "to allow myself to be a doormat." Hence the masochistic person cannot permit himself to close the books on old grievances; indeed, he feels that he should not, even when he might actually be tempted to do so.

For example, a woman who was frequently preoccupied by her husband's hurtful acts of inconsiderateness, was greatly tempted to allow a recent incident to pass. They had planned to go to a party, and she was looking forward to enjoying it and tempted to make peace. But she had no sooner noticed this temptation than she reminded herself once again how hurt she was. She reminded herself that she could not "simply forget" such hurtful and unfair treatment, that she could not "sweep my feelings under the rug," and she began once again to cry. This vacillation was repeated several times.

The masochistic nursing and exaggeration of suffering does not merely prolong or reproduce the experience of that suffering. It is an action that changes the individual's relationship to that experience from a passive to a more active one. One "faces" the experience: that is, one recognizes it for what it is —defeat, humiliation, injustice; it is noted, marked down, as one would who has further reckoning to do. This is the action of someone who, however limited his power, is not prepared to yield. If it does not provide a moral victory, at least it makes a charge. It accuses the offender by pointing to his victim; it keeps alive in the mind's record an injustice committed, a score unsettled. Thus, again, such masochistic nursing and exaggeration of suffering is not at all a reflection of passivity or acquiescence, or—as it is sometimes described—a "wallowing" in defeat. Quite the contrary. It is no pleasure to the masochistic person either, on the whole; it is a necessity, a principled act of will, from which he cannot release himself without losing his self-respect and feeling more deeply and finally defeated, humiliated, and powerless.

Everyone is familiar with the self-depreciation of some masochistic people. They express it typically in continual and exaggerated admissions of inadequacy or insufficiency of one kind or another. For example, "I know I'm not smart," "I know I'm a boring person," "You must get tired of listening to people like me," "I must be a burden to you."

These admissions are as a rule presented as though in a spirit of frank, even conscientious humility, a spirit of facing the facts. They are intended to be taken as an apology or a humble appeal for tolerance. But there is something strange about such appeals for tolerance, something that sets them apart from genuine humility and even makes them discomforting to hear. What is presented as a conscientious frankness and humility sounds artificial, forced, overdone, and actually contains a defensive attitude. The exaggeration of his deference and the unnecessarily harsh, even cruelly disdainful attitude toward himself that the masochistic person ascribes to the other one reflect his consciousness of what he presumes to be an unequal relationship and the other's claims to superiority. It is the presumption of such a relationship and such claims that prompts the masochistic person to anticipate and to face them unflinchingly. By anticipating and exaggerating this inequality, by exaggerating his own inadequacy and anticipating the other's claims to superiority, he neutralizes the impact of those claims and defeats them. He defeats the humiliation of this inequality by his exaggerated humility; he defeats insult by the prior admission of inadequacy; he defeats rebuff by withdrawing any claims to acceptance. In some instances, this defensiveness becomes quite conscious and especially sharp; the exaggerations reach the point of caricature—"Pardon me for living" —and become frankly ironic. By the patent exaggeration of his own humility and of the other's superiority, in other words, the masochistic person casts doubt on the inequality and hints at the other's pretensions.

The self-evident moral superiority of frankness and humility over smugness and pretension might also be called a moral victory. More important, the masochistic person has transformed what might otherwise have been an experience of shame and humiliation before the presumed superiority of others, into an experience of comparative strength and a certain dignity.

Another version of this process occurs when the masochistic individual has already actually experienced the impact of a humiliating rebuff, insult, or defeat and attempts to regain dignity after the fact by siezing the insult and inflicting an exaggerated version of it on himself, again sometimes ironically. A striking instance occurs in the case of a masochistic young woman extensively described by Brenman. This sensitive and prideful patient was taken aback by her boyfriend's teasing. She described the event to her therapist as follows:

We were looking at an old yearbook. . . . I tried to hide the book so he wouldn't see my picture. I looked so awful. He took it from me, looked at it and said, "My but you were a fat blob last year." That was too much . . . this really got me. I rushed off and wrote a long letter to him describing in detail how ugly I not only was last year but am now, what a beastly personality I have and too bad he hadn't found me out sooner. It hurt him terribly—I never saw anybody so devastated.[13]

Much masochistic self-depreciation and deference has, as I mentioned, an ironic quality, which is unusually frank and bitter in this example. Almost all such self-depreciation contains at least some suggestion of irony. There is a simple reason for this. The essential device of irony, the discrediting of a thesis or the expression of its opposite by exaggerating it, is closely akin to the defensive device of exaggeration of all masochistic self-depreciation. There is an affinity between the atti-

[13]Margaret Brenman, "On Teasing and Being Teased: And the Problem of Moral Masochism," *The Psychoanalytic Study of the Child* (New York: International Universities Press, 1952), vol. VII, p. 279.

tudes that give rise to each. The device of irony, on account of its ambiguity, is a natural weapon of the less powerful against the more powerful, as masochistic self-depreciation is a natural defense. It is not difficult to understand, therefore, the easy emergence of irony from such self-depreciation when the defensiveness of that self-depreciation is intensified.

These principles also apply to the exaggeratedly abject concessions and admissions of all kinds of culpability and personal failings, beyond mere inadequacy, that masochistic people make, sometimes even inflicting physical punishment on themselves with the insistence that it is deserved. (Brenman's patient, for example, stood unprotected before an open window on freezing nights and kept herself awake to the point of exhaustion, stating that she didn't deserve to sleep.)[14] There is a difference between the attitude of admission and confession that mainly characterizes this behavior and an attitude of repentance or contrition. Repentance and the sense of guilt involve an internal judgment of one's action ("I shouldn't have . . ."); admission, on the other hand, is an act of yielding, a concession, to presumed judgment, a submission to punishment. The masochistic person seems ready to concede every charge, to acknowledge every kind of failing, to admit that he deserves, and to accept, any punishment. These forced and exaggerated, unmistakably artificial, admissions are not prompted by guilt. Guilt, a sensation of internal judgment, seems largely transformed by the self-consciousness of the masochistic person into a sense of exposure, shame, and vulnerability to humiliation; these are the sensations that prompt such exaggerated admissions and abject pleas of guilt. It is this sense of shame and exposure that prompts a determined, unflinching, and, finally, defensively exaggerated self-exposure

[14]Ibid., p. 43.

and is relieved by that self-exposure. It is a self-exposure, and sometimes a self-punishment, that outdoes all possible judgments in what it concedes and in its abjectness. It is capable of replacing shame not merely with a sense of moral superiority but with a martyr's pride.

If this understanding of masochism is correct, the masochistic individual shares with other rigid characters the same will and determination, the same concerns with dignity, the same or similar concerns with giving in. In the masochistic case, however, all these have a special tendency: a defensive tendency, not absent in rigid characters generally, but especially pronounced here and of a special sort. It is the particular defensiveness of the rigid character who experiences himself as, or who actually is, in an inferior, weaker, or subordinate position, facing unequal circumstances or superior forces. It is the defensiveness of the individual whose self-respect is less able to tolerate the impact of such circumstances than another might be; hence, of the individual who is, often bitterly, preoccupied with personal inequity, with being victimized, demeaned, or humiliated, and who is unable to—or, rather, is determined not to—reconcile himself to such experiences and assimilate them.

Masochistic people anticipate or reproduce the impact of superior forces in such a way as to diminish it.[15] Such behavior is not therefore "self-destructive," as it is often described; on

---

[15]Theodor Reik emphasized the anticipation process in masochism (*Masochism in Modern Man* [New York: Farrar & Straus, 1941]). My conclusion about the defensive nature of masochism is a more general statement of his view of masochism as essentially an anticipation of punishment, a "flight forward," as he calls it. The location of the basis of this process in the defensive attitudes of the rigid character permits a more general understanding of it. For example, the defensive masochistic reaction anticipates not merely punishment but also humiliation, exposure, and so on. Also, as I have shown, that defensive reaction, the exaggerated outdoing, is not limited to anticipation or to a "flight forward"; it may also be a response to the impact of past humiliation or exposure.

the contrary, it is self-protective. If masochism is regarded only from the standpoint of its subject matter, its themes, the content of its preoccupation and its behavior, it would be easy to conclude that it is self-destructive, a surrender to pain and suffering, humiliation, inadequacy, and cruelty because these are its constant concerns. If, however, one takes account of the attitudes with which these themes are expressed, of the will with which they are confronted, then one sees a picture not of the individual who surrenders but of the one who concedes territory on his own terms precisely in order to avoid surrender.

Masochism and Paranoia

It has been observed by Bak and Brenman, among others, that masochism is closely associated with paranoia or at least with projective mechanisms, although there is theoretical disagreement about the nature of that association. From the standpoint of studying paranoia, Bak[16] has suggested that masochism (here considered as a libidinal tendency) plays a critical role in paranoia; whereas from the standpoint of studying masochism, Brenman[17] concludes that projective mechanisms are a regular element of masochism. Although Brenman's view, in this respect, is closer to my own and, I believe, more explanatory, a certain case can actually be made in each direction. The reason is that both masochism and paranoia are special cases of rigid character; they share many general tendencies, and there is no doubt that manifestations of each are likely to appear in the predominant context of the other. I am referring especially to the defensive attitudes and special sensitivities to

[16]Robert C. Bak, "Masochism in Paranoia," *Psychoanalytic Quarterly* 15:285–301.
[17]"On Teasing and Being Teased" [13].

superior authority, coercion, and so forth, that are central to both masochistic and paranoid conditions and are only potential—for example, in the form of stubbornness—in compulsive characters. This relationship, and the relationship between this defensive sensitivity and projection, will become more clear in the later chapter on paranoid rigidity.

Masochism and Women

The psychoanalytic idea of masochism as an intrinsically female tendency has been challenged—properly—as tainted with male chauvinism. The idea is objectionable on two counts: first, it suggests that it is characteristic of women to find satisfaction in being dominated and even in being coerced; second, it contains the notion that a submissiveness of this supposed kind is rooted in female biology. That such a conception is convenient to a male-dominated society seems obvious. Nevertheless, clinical evidence is convincing, not that women in general are masochistic, but that among masochistic individuals there is a predominance of women. In the light of the analysis of masochism that I have proposed, such a relationship does not seem at all remarkable. As I said, masochism is, among rigid characters, characteristic of those who experience themselves as being, and often are, in comparatively powerless or subordinate positions. Such in general are the experiences and the circumstances of women. Therefore, the identification of masochism as a female tendency reflects, not a female satisfaction in submission, but rather the tendency of women who are rigid characters to defend their autonomy and protect their dignity in this pseudo-submissive way.

Masochism and Sadism

The picture I have drawn of masochism and sadism departs
from the usual psychoanalytic one of the correspondence between them: of the latter, as an impulse to inflict suffering on
others; of the former, as an impulse to inflict it on oneself—
alternative turnings in the direction of a single impulse. My
picture suggests a kinship of a different and more complicated
sort. Each disposition involves, in its own way, a defensive,
usually angry assertion of will; each is driven by a sense of
inferiority, shame, or humiliation; each is deeply and self-consciously concerned with relative position, rank, and measure,
with superiority and inferiority—but the sadistic person from
the superior position, and the masochistic person from the
inferior one. There is no doubt that the two are distinguishable
and general tendencies of character, but their kinship is such
that it is not difficult to understand the typical existence of
both tendencies in the same individual, their relative promi-
nence even varying to a certain extent with different circumstances.

Chapter 6

Sexual Sadism and Masochism

THE PSYCHOANALYTIC VIEW of sexual cruelty involves two factors: an early fixation on a sadistic—that is, cruel or aggressive—or masochistic component of infantile sexuality; and the exaggeration in the adult of this aggressive interest and its recombination with genital sexuality as a reassurance against sexual (castration) anxiety or guilt.[1] It is the second factor that contains the problem. No one can reasonably doubt—whatever his view of the libido theory—that adult sexual interests have sources in the retained tendencies of childhood interests and sensuality—in this case, the aggressiveness and cruelty of childhood. The problem is not merely to identify sources and com-

[1]For a detailed discussion of the psychoanalytic view, see Otto Fenichel, *The Psychoanalytic Theory of Neurosis* (New York: W.W. Norton, 1945), pp. 354–65. Also Sigmund Freud, "A Child Is Being Beaten," *Collected Papers* vol. II (London: Hogarth Press and Institute of Psychoanalysis, 1919).

ponents of the adult sexual interest, but to understand their significance for its ultimate subjective quality.

The attempt to understand sado-masochism in this way, as a compound of sexual excitement and aggression, does not, it seems to me, explain the subjective qualities of sexual cruelty. Thus, the aggressiveness of sadism is thought to reassure the sadist that he is not himself the passive victim of aggression; while the masochist's experience as the victim of actual aggression is thought to forestall his guilt and allay his fear of punishment.[2] This explanation of aggression as a *condition* for sexual expression, however, does not explain at all how cruelty acquires its own intense erotic value.[3] For that is the central subjective fact: for certain individuals cruelty does not merely permit sexual excitement or relieve sexual anxiety, but intensifies sexual excitement and is exciting in itself.

The same point can be made in connection with the sense of power which has been thought to be a component of sexual sadism and also a reassurance against sexual anxiety. Something of the reverse is also held concerning sadism: namely, that the sexual relationship allows one to experience power. The central question is left unsatisfied by these ideas. If power relationships —subjugation, coercion, and so on—are crucially involved in sexual sadism—as they clearly are—what is it about these cruel relationships, and about cruelty in general, that is, for certain individuals, not merely reassuring or satisfying in a subsidiary way but intrinsically exciting?

---

[2]Theodor Reik, *Masochism in Modern Man* (New York: Farrar & Straus, 1941).
[3]Fenichel concedes this point (Theory of Neurosis [1], p.354) and relies on the proposition of the original fixation to explain the intrinsic erotic value of cruelty for the adult. But this explanation again, it seems to me, skirts the essential question of the intensification of that erotic value in adult sadism.

Pain and Eroticism

There is good reason to think that the relation of pain to sexual excitement has a certain biological basis. Freud[4] and numerous others have noted that certain kinds of pain, especially cutaneous pain, is closely akin to erotic sensation and easily spills over into it. Biting and scratching are a common part of foreplay and, according to Ford and Beach,[5] are particularly so in societies where children and adolescents are customarily permitted greater sexual freedom. Beach points out, furthermore, that sensations of pain—such as those produced by biting—are regularly associated with sexual arousal among many species of animals. Altogether, there is, he says, hardly any doubt "that any man or woman is physiologically capable of positive erotic responses to mild degrees of pain."[6]

This proximity between sexual excitement and certain painful sensations seems related to another fundamental fact: that a certain degree of forceful contact is part of much sexual activity. That is, at least a mild degree of forceful body contact is involved in the creation of the sensations of sexual excitement—not only the skin sensations created by pressure and friction, but also the deeper body sensations. It is pertinent also that a certain degree of physical force or violence is involved in many kinds of sensual satisfaction and physical pleasure apart from sexual activity. Babies enjoy and are relaxed by not only rocking but also by jiggling or rhythmic bouncing movements, sometimes surprisingly vigorous ones. Adults enjoy

[4]Sigmund Freud, *Three Essays on the Theory of Sexuality* (London: Hogarth Press, 1949 [originally published 1905]), p. 81.
[5]Clellan S. Ford and Frank A. Beach, *Patterns of Sexual Behavior* (New York: Harper & Bros. and Paul B. Hoeber, 1951), p. 64.
[6]Ibid., p. 65.

many kinds of violent or forceful exercise and sports and force-ful massage.

We should not, therefore, dismiss too quickly as trivial or superficial the sado-masochistic person's own view of the na-ture of his sexual interest in pain and physical violence. In his view they intensify the sensual experience, hence the sexual excitement. Psychologists assert that he uses sex to satisfy aims of aggression or power; he says the reverse, that he uses violence and force to achieve sexual aims. Psychologists assume that pain and violence are conditions for sexual expression; he says that they are themselves erotic. Psychologists assume that his interest in violence and pain is essentially symbolic; he says that his interest in them is sensual, and that where it is symbolic, it is symbolic of sensuality. He maintains that the intensity of erotic excitement and physical pleasure is, up to a point at least, directly related to the intensity and effectiveness of force and violence, because pain is the most intense form of sensual arousal.

This, at least, is Sade's own view as a highly conscious and purposeful, not to say principled, sensualist. He says:

> It is simply a matter of jangling all our nerves with the most violent possible shock. Now, since there can be no doubt that pain affects us more strongly than pleasure, when this sensation is produced in others, our very being will vibrate more vigorously with the resulting shocks.[7]

One should not disdain the obvious. If we take it as a first fact that an aim of sado-masochism is sensual and erotic excite-ment or its intensification through pain and violence, we have at least a starting point and a direction for further questions.

[7]Quoted in Simone de Beauvoir, *The Marquis de Sade (Must We Burn Sade?)* (New York: Grove Press, 1953), p. 31.

Why, for certain individuals particularly, should pain and violence have such an effect? Why such a special interest, as it sometimes seems, in the intensification of sensual experience at all? There are further questions: how to understand the sado-masochistic interest in and excitement by various kinds of cruelty which are actually far removed from physical pain or violence and, indeed, from sensuality, such as humiliation and sexual degradation. These questions cannot be answered by studying only the sado-masochistic act or the sado-masochistic drive. They are questions not so much about a kind of drive as about a kind of mind or a kind of person.

Detachment in Sadism

Considering their typical consciousness of sensuality and, in some cases like Sade's, even emphatic advocacy of sensuality, sado-masochistic sexual attitudes often seem remarkably detached. This detachment has been noted by several writers but especially clearly by Beauvoir in the example of her study of Sade.

She says: "Never in his stories does sensual pleasure appear as self-forgetfulness, swooning or abandoned."[8] She speaks of Sade as "a will bent on fulfilling the flesh without losing itself in it,"[9] and of the sexual act itself, for Sade, as "a spectacle which one observes from a distance at the same time that one is performing it."[10]

[8] Ibid., p. 32.
[9] Ibid., p. 39.
[10] Ibid., p. 43.

It is all true. Sade's characters—I am not referring here merely to the detachment of the writer himself—arrange and perform the scene of sexual excitement with great deliberateness, concentrating on creating certain effects. They, particularly the male characters, observe themselves during the performance or sometimes observe while others perform; they are aroused by observing the pain of one woman while being physically relieved by another or, having arranged the tableau, they simply observe with excitement and do not participate at all.

The enjoyment of the spectacle of sensuality in contrast to sensual enjoyment itself, or the intensification of sensual enjoyment and excitement by the simultaneous, perhaps greater, excitement of its spectacle, is typical of sado-masochism. This enjoyment is evident in the interest in watching one's own sexual activity, in photographing it, in describing it especially in "dirty" language, or in hearing it described while participating in it. These are means to intensify excitement not through erotic sensuality but through the *idea* of erotic sensuality. They intensify sex with the more exciting idea of "sexiness." They use the actual experience to compose a pornographic tableau. Contrary to the usual human tendency, the function of the action is to facilitate the fantasy.

Sado-masochistic arrangements have something of the quality of theatrical productions. Whips, leather, the paraphernalia of sensuality and subjugation, are used essentially to create the erotic idea. Whips are not used only to produce pain; they are used more as props for the fantasy of pain and violence and the idea of erotic sensuality. Hence their use is accompanied by exaggerated expressions of pain. The pain may be small, but the writhing is great. The partner as well is not merely an object for physical, sensual use but is also, perhaps primarily, a prop, an aid to the imagining of a scene of erotic sensuality. Altogether, sado-masochistic sexuality is a highly ideational matter, far more a product of the imagination than of the senses. It may include, in the event and even in the fantasy, little actual physical contact or none at all. Its excitement is over ideas and symbols of erotic sensuality, especially in the most concentrated, exaggerated forms (leather, whips, pain, and so on). This is what Beauvoir means by "the will bent on fulfilling the flesh without losing itself in it." It is a purposeful sexuality, a sexuality of the will, not an abandoned sexuality of the senses. In short, it is in various degrees a form of sexuality consistent with rigid character.

The Erotic Theme

The nature of rigid character—its regime of will, discipline, authority, its moralistic prejudices—has further consequences for the nature of sexual interests. Moralistic notions of sex as dirty, coarse, and degrading may have the effect not merely of inhibiting sexual interests but of making dirtiness, coarseness, and degradation especially erotic. Similarly, the exclusion of erotic sensuality from the interests, attachments, and affections of regular, "proper," life may have the effect of making especially erotic those exotic figures or relationships that are unencumbered by affection. Above all, the rigid views of sexual responsiveness and sexual excitement as inimical to self-control, and of the sexual relationship as a surrender of one to the other, will have the effect of imbuing ideas and images of wantonness and subjugation—images of the prostitute and the slave, for example—with special erotic significance. The very conditions that are abhorred by rigid characters are highly erotic, and for the same reason that they are abhorred: they are experienced as antithetical or inimical to the regime of the will, to self-control and self-discipline; they signify surrender of the will, abandonment of self-control, restraint, propriety, and dignity.

There is no doubt that ideas of subjugation, of relationships of coercion and surrender, cruel power and humiliating obedience, and innumerable variations of these comprise the basic erotic theme, the basic sexual situation, of sado-masochistic fantasies. All the other elements—the inflicting of pain, struggle against restraint, and so on—are merely sensual particulars or embellishments of this basic situation. For the sado-masochistic person, ideas and images of such relationships are suffused with eroticism. In order to understand this fact more clearly, it is helpful to remember that the rigid will is, so to speak, engaged on two fronts, internal and external. That is, the rigid individual is concerned with self-control, self-discipline, with not giving in to himself—and also with not giving in to others. He is stubborn, defensive of his authority, pridefully sensitive to humiliation or coercion from above, authoritarian and contemptuous toward those below. In his picture of the sexual relationship, these two kinds of giving in—to the self in the form of sexual excitement, and to the other—are particularly closely related, and both kinds of surrender or abrogation of the will are involved: each implies the other.

To the individual, in other words, whose will is invested in not giving in to others or in making others give in to him, the erotic idea of sensuality and sexual excitement in the sexual relationship is also an idea of the surrender of one to another, the giving in of one to the sexual excitement aroused by the other, of the collapse of the will of one to resist the other, of the humiliation and degradation of one by the other. Hence, this becomes the erotic, the "sexy," image of the sexual relationship. The sexual relationship consists of one being "fucked" or "screwed" by the other; and it is exactly this idea of one being "fucked" or "screwed" by the other that becomes erotic. The relation between the two kinds of surrender of the will is contained in many sado-masochistic fantasies in which, say, the aloof woman, once sexually aroused, becomes the abject sexual slave of the one who arouses her; she is "crazy with desire" and begs to be satisfied, to be used. The converse is also familiar in sado-masochistic fantasies: the subjugation of the victim, the overpowering of her will to resist, of her dignity and restraint, awakens her own overpowering sexual urges, and so on. In the context of these ideas, any image or representation of the condition of subjugation, any action that suggests abjectness on the part of one party, for example, or action on the part of the other which suggests contempt, contemptuous punishment, or "discipline" intensifies the erotic quality of a sexual situation.

All of this eroticism, I must emphasize again, remains essentially in the realm of ideas and fantasies and of the symbolic actions and arrangements that facilitate them. It is to the rigid person—to whom the *actuality* of sexual abandonment is inimical to the will, to self-control, and to self-respect—that the *idea* of subjugation seems so erotic.

I have so far hardly distinguished between sadistic and masochistic sexual interests; for the most part, what I have said applies as well to the one as to the other. It is a fact that in many aspects of their essential nature the two can hardly be distinguished and for many purposes can best be regarded as a single form of sexual interest and not merely as two complementary forms. For example, the directions of the two interests are not as opposite as might be imagined; it is not quite the case that the one is an excitement at the idea of subjugation and humiliation and the other at the idea of power. In reality, both are interests in the erotic ideas and images of subjugation, humiliation, pain, and so on. The primary focus of *both* kinds of erotic interest is the *victim* of cruelty, the one who is subjugated, humiliated, and experiencing the pain, rather than the one who inflicts it. This is the principal locale of the erotic action, of actual physical sensation (as through whips or binding), of the erotic surrender of will, and therefore of erotic interest. Let me refer again to the remark of Sade that I quoted before. Speaking of the erotic value of pain from the sadistic point of view, he says: "When this sensation *is produced in others,* our very being will vibrate more vigorously" (my emphasis).

If sadism and masochism share a single form of sexual interest, their differences may be reduced to the alternative points of view that this picture of the sexual relationship and of human relationships in general allows that interest to take— that of the superior and that of the subordinate position. For the person in the weaker or subordinate position (most commonly, though not necessarily, the female), it is the idea of her (or his) own will-less surrender, subjugation, or degradation that is erotic. For the person in the superior position, who may be characterized generally by attitudes of exaggerated authority and contempt for the weak and subordinate, it is the idea of the other's abjectness. Each in his way seeks to create an erotically degraded, subjugated, and will-less image of the subordinate one and in fact both fantasies are, typically, to some extent erotic to each person.

The fact that from the sadistic standpoint the idea of the other's debasement and subjugation is erotic, and from the masochistic standpoint, the idea of one's own, may have further consequences. Masochistic fantasy may well be more erotic for certain rigid characters but at the same time conflictful and repugnant in ways that sadistic interest is not. Such conflict occurs, probably, especially among rigid men for whom the erotic image may be of the subjugated woman.[11] But it may occur also, for example, in some rigid, prideful women in connection with prostitute fantasies. In sadism, such conflict is avoided. The idea of the *other's* sexual degradation or subjugation is in no way shameful or an offense to pride; on the contrary, it simply means that the figure of sexual interest will be regarded with contempt. Just such feelings seem to characterize the sexual attitudes of many rigid men—and even a certain conception of "manliness."

---

[11]See, for example, the case of Schreber discussed in the following chapter, pp. 146–66.

Chapter 7

Paranoid Rigidity

IF ONE MAY SPEAK of two aspects of individual autonomy—the internal processes of self-direction, on the one hand, and the individual's relations with external authority, on the other—then obsessive-compulsive neurosis can be described as primarily a pathology of the first, and paranoid conditions of the second. The distinction is not absolute, but in general where rigidity of volitional direction and control is particularly severe, the struggles of will that in the compulsive case are experienced as internal are replaced by struggles of will with certain external figures, especially with figures of authority or rank or with institutions that have a certain degree of coercive power. These relationships become defensive and antagonistic and the individual's concerns about them, about their threat to autonomy or to personal authority, become preoccupying. This is the specific, most characteristic nature of paranoid concerns, although they are often described merely as concerns with threatened aggression.

Thus, the nonpsychotic paranoid individual typically is constantly concerned about being "pushed around" or humiliated, about infringements on his rights or affronts to his dignity, about issues of rank—who is subordinate and who is in charge —and so on. The same issues are more acutely expressed in such typical paranoid delusions as a feeling of being threatened by powerful coercive agencies such as "the communists" or by supernatural forces or devices (such as rays, influencing machines, poisons, or hypnosis) that can control the body or violate it or can control or weaken the will. While the compulsive person's will—his rules and regulations, self-discipline, will power, and so on—is directed against himself—against laziness, waste of time, and self-indulgence—the paranoid will, in such forms as guardedness and suspiciousness, is mobilized against an external threat to its authority.

There is no doubt that paranoid rigidity is the more severe. If the compulsive person is stubborn and difficult to influence, the guarded, paranoid individual is more so. The rigidity of thinking that is contained in the fixed biases of paranoid suspiciousness, even when it has not reached delusional proportions, is of a more severe order, more impervious to objective contradiction than is, for example, mere dogmatism. Even the deliberateness and carefulness of movement of the guarded paranoid individual—the steering of the body, of gesture and facial expression—is more extreme.

Why should rigidity take this particular and more severe, defensive form? Why, in these cases, should the experience of the threat to autonomy and personal authority shift to an external arena from an internal one? One answer to these questions is the defense mechanism of projection: that paranoid defensive rigidity—suspiciousness, guardedness, and the like—is in response to, follows upon, the projection onto other figures of unconscious feelings, impulses or ideas, particularly aggressive ones.

There are serious problems with this answer. The process of projection understood in any simple way—that is, as an "expulsion" of feelings onto others—does not explain the case. I shall discuss this in more detail in a moment. It is enough to mention now that the paranoid experience of threat—its intrinsic aspect of self-reference, the direction of antagonism (in subjective experience) from external object back to subject, not to mention the specific nature of the experience of threatened autonomy—is not actually explained by a simple process of expulsion onto others of one's own unconscious feelings, impulses, or ideas. Apart from this, projection cannot be regarded as an elementary mechanism whose appearance needs no further explanation. It is a complicated process, and there remains in any case the problem of explaining its origins in the psychological makeup of these particular individuals, its appearance under particular subjective conditions.

Paranoid experience, and the process of projection as well, become more comprehensible if the relationship of rigidity and defensiveness to projection is understood differently—in part the other way around. I shall try to show that it is an intrinsic characteristic of rigidity of self-direction, when it reaches a certain degree of severity, to give rise to a defensive and antagonistic relationship with the external world. Given this, the processes of projection and the nature of projective distortion immediately become more comprehensible. Projective distortions, the imagination and anticipation of various kinds of external threat to autonomy and personal authority—slights, humiliations, coercive efforts of various kinds, and so on—can then be understood not as the cause of defensiveness but, on the contrary, as its result. From this standpoint, in other words, the projective identification of the enemy in the shadows can be seen as the product of a nervous, defensively searching and anticipating—suspicious—attention. Once the paranoid person has identified the threat, there is a further mobilization—an intensification of guardedness, suspiciousness, defensive antagonism—against it.

Rigidity and Defensiveness

In general the extent to which an individual can exercise personal authority may be limited by various external conditions, in particular by the presence of some coercive or even benign superior authority. It follows from this fact alone and prior to any projective distortion that the attitude toward such authority held by certain rigid individuals—people of especially rigid will and the self-conscious, exaggerated, and essentially uncertain sense of their own authority and dignity that is often associated with a rigid will—will be defensive and antagonistic. This is exactly what we see in the paranoid character. The paranoid person—often grandiose and arrogant though underneath feeling ashamed and small, determined to be strong and to be "on top of things," though underneath feeling weak—is constantly, pridefully, concerned with those who, on account of their rank or superior authority, can make him feel small and powerless. He is extremely conscious of status and rank, of the boss. Figures of authority, after all, loom large to those who underneath feel small even if they do not recognize that they feel small. The paranoid person is grudgingly, unwillingly, conscious of such authority, pridefully sensitive to criticism from such figures and the possibility of humiliation by them, determined not to give in.

For example, one such man could not bring himself to address his superiors at work by the title "Mr." He refused, as he put it, to "crawl" or "jump through the hoop." Similarly, he could not bring himself to address his therapist as "Dr." even at their first meeting and used from the outset what he assumed was the therapist's nickname.

The paranoid individual is constantly engaged in such defensive and antagonistic relationships—at least subjectively and often objectively as well—with the boss, the supervisor, or even the neighbor who, by erecting a fence in the wrong place, has aroused his determination not to be "pushed around." These are, from a subjective standpoint, struggles of will. The rigid will of the paranoid individual, in contrast to the compulsive person's dutiful application to productive purposes and accomplishments, is largely absorbed in such struggles.

This defensiveness and absorption in such struggles of will exists, it should be remembered, prior to projection. Although some degree of projective distortion is usually involved in the ultimate image of the external figure, it is not essential to the basic defensiveness. That defensiveness is a product of a rigidity more extreme and at the same time less stable than the compulsive person's. The paranoid individual, like the compulsive, is under the sway of authoritative images and standards —images and standards of what he should be; but his identification of himself with these images and standards is even less successful, less complete, and the disparity and tension between them and his experience of himself is greater. Hence, the acute feelings of inferiority, shame, and weakness that are always at the edge of his consciousness; and, at the same time, the exaggerated and self-conscious assertions of authority and competence, the rigidity of will and sensitive pride, and the preoccupation with the defense of these particularly before figures whom he actually respects more than he respects himself.

It is not only such more or less direct threats to their authority and self-respect as may be contained in the presence of a superior that excites such people to defensiveness and antagonism. Their guardedness is likely to be aroused by almost any abrupt change, anything unexpected, unfamiliar, or ambiguous, anything that contains the possibility of surprise. Is this only a result of projective apprehension, or is it, again, a process whose basis is prior to projection?

Actually, all rigid characters are discomforted by the new, the changing, even the moderately unpredictable. For this reason, many compulsive people arrange their lives according to routine, mark off a niche within which they can live in an orderly and regulated way, protected from change or novelty. In this—or simply on account of the internal rules, regulations, and steady purposes by which they live—they seem imperturbable and stolid. By contrast, paranoid individuals might easily be described as hyperperturbable, sensitive, and reactive to the slightest unusualness. Actually, the two modes are not so disparate. They are both responses of rigid self-direction and self-control—perhaps the nervous worry of obsessional people who brace themselves for bad news at every unexpected telephone call or letter is an intermediate mode—to events that are not already assimilated and therefore threaten that direction and control. The compulsive person of rigid and stable purpose can withstand—that is, he can ignore as distractions—the surprises and instabilities of daily life. But the rigid character who is less stable, less certain of purpose and personal authority, more tense, is more perturbable and, being perturbable, must be alert to, anticipate, gain some sense of mastery over the unexpected, that which might frighten or confuse him, make him feel small, helpless, or vulnerable.

Such people may try to avoid unfamiliar surroundings. One man avoided unfamiliar restaurants or stores where, on account of his uncertainty about proper behavior, he might be "humiliated." More commonly, these people may assume an exaggerated and artificial attitude of self-confidence in unfamiliar circumstances.

In other words, the existence of a certain degree of instability in rigid character will inevitably give rise, even before projection, to a sense of vulnerability and to a guarded and, ultimately, defensive and antagonistic relationship to various aspects of the world. It is probably true, however, that projection is never altogether absent when that anxiety reaches a certain level or when the tactics and exigencies of defensive efforts become absorbing concerns.

Thus the artificial attitude of self-confidence in unfamiliar surroundings may in more rigid and defensive individuals become an attitude of "I know what you're up to." A more extreme, clearly projective, form of this attitude was expressed by a patient who, at the outset of his first visit to a therapist's office, said, "I assume you're recording this. It's all right with me, go right ahead."

Projection

In the context of existing defensive attitudes and concerns, the process of projection is less difficult to understand. It begins with the intensification of those defensive concerns as a consequence of some further threat, internal or external in origin, to self-respect or autonomy.

For example, a rather grave, dignified middle-aged man disapproves of his own solitary drinking and is ashamed of it; on the day following an evening of drinking, he feels especially self-conscious before his associates at work and his superiors, although he is able to do his work perfectly well and there are no obvious signs of last night's bout.

In the rigid, defensive individual many kinds of internal conflicts with the demands and standards of the will may have such effects. Because such a person is engaged in a struggle against threat to his self-respect and the authority of his will on two fronts, the internal and the external, any further loss of self-respect that originates internally will intensify his sense of vulnerability to external threat as well. Thus, an experience of failure or a business mistake that intensifies his sense of insufficiency will also immediately intensify his self-conscious-ness, shame, and sense of vulnerability to exposure, blame, or humiliation.

One rigid man, already self-conscious before his boss, feels nervous and bold asking for a raise; he gets it, but immedi-ately becomes concerned that the boss will not like his ag-gressiveness. Another man, already concerned about defend-ing his rights, accepts a smaller raise than he had expected; he feels he has been "weak" and becomes concerned that he has been taken advantage of.

In such ways, the intensification of internal conflict gives rise to an intensification of defensive sensitivity to external figures. The process we call projection goes farther than such defensive sensitivity but is a product of it. When internal tension intensifies defensive tension, the defensive mobilization becomes more rigid. Sensitivities become more acute, more anticipatory, and more rigidly biased in their anticipations. The individual is no longer merely sensitive to the possibility of a slight, for example, but expects it and looks for it, even obsessively. He does not want it to escape him if it should be present. He regards its apparent absence as inconclusive and is satisfied only when he has discovered evidence of it. This rigid bias marks the transformation of defensive sensitivity into what we call suspiciousness. The nature of the individual's particular bias and expectancy corresponds, of course, to the nature of his defensive concerns. The product of such bias is projection.

A competent and well-respected man who was, however, not convinced of his own competency and was concerned about his status in the firm, made a mistake in his work. It was not of great consequence, could be easily corrected, and was unlikely to be noticed by anyone else. Nevertheless, for some days afterward, he was preoccupied with the possibility of its being discovered and the humiliation that would follow. On one occasion, he "noticed" the boss glance at him in passing, and thought the boss was thinking, "This man is the weak link in our organization."

In projection, the individual regards the external figure of defensive concern with such tension and absorption and such rigid bias and expectancy that the "discovery" of a threat corresponding to the nature of the defensive concern is inevitable. The individual, in other words, loses detachment from the object of his defensive concern. That figure is no longer an objective figure. A few compliant features, significant clues, are enough to precipitate out of defensive bias and expectancy a threatening image or idea that is essentially a creation of that bias and expectancy. All that is not compliant with that bias, the individual brushes aside, disdains as inessential. At the same time, absorbed by his defensive concern and rigidly mobilized, his consciousness of his own internal conflict is sharply diminished or disappears. Thus, what was originally an internal threat to self-respect is transformed by the workings of rigid and defensive character into an external threat to self-respect.

Contrary to what one might easily assume, the content of projective ideas is by no means necessarily the same as the content of the internal threat it may be said to have replaced. Projective ideas are not merely "expulsions" of unconscious thoughts or feelings onto external figures but extensions of the defensive relationship with such figures. Accordingly, these ideas are determined not directly by the feelings that intensified that defensiveness but by the particular defensive concerns and anticipations that are excited. Sometimes the relationship between the two is simple, and the translation relatively direct; but sometimes it is not simple.

Thus it would be absurd to imagine—and no one does—that the projectively experienced threat of being trapped reflects a repudiated impulse to trap. Such projective ideas or concerns with other forms of coercion may, however, easily arise in the mind of a rigid and guarded person who is tempted, in one way or another, to drop his guard, to "give in," or to "go soft."

For example, a female patient in her twenties, in an open and voluntary psychiatric institution, was ordinarily guarded and aloof, if not frankly antagonistic, in her relations with the institution's staff. On certain occasions, however, she was clearly tempted to relax her guardedness, to "admit" that she enjoyed some institutional activity, to do something she thought might please her therapist, or to lose interest in her constant plans to quit the place. Such occasions were regularly followed by her realization that there were plans to "trap" her there, to brainwash her, or in some way to induce her to surrender.

When the content of projective ideas is actually essentially the same as the content of the original internal concern—as in so-called superego projection where self-critical ideas or self-doubt is projectively attributed to others—there is a special reason. In these cases, the form of the original internal experience, a self-critical judgment, happens to be identical with the form of the later defensive concern. The original internal tension, in other words, is already a critical self-consciousness; the individual already feels in a quasi-defensive position before himself; and the defensive concern or projective idea generated involves only the substitution of an external figure for the individual's own self-consciousness. Thus the projective idea, "This man is the weak link in our organization." Or the projective idea, in a paranoid man much concerned with manliness and strength, that various people in public places are looking at him as though he were a homosexual.

The reason that projective ideas are not unlimited in variety is also a reflection of the fact that they are not simple "expulsions" of unconscious mental contents but are the products of the defensive concerns of rigid characters. These ideas are largely limited to certain closely related themes that reflect such concerns. Thus, defensive concerns with exposure to humiliation or contempt give rise to projective ideas of being seen, noticed, regarded as "the weak link," as effeminate, and so on—or, especially among those who may be more arrogant or grandiose, suspicions of slights or insults to their authority or status. Those who may be more rigid and therefore more estranged from their own internal conflict and their own anxiety about weakness, softness, or "giving in" (to themselves or others) in abhorrent ways may develop ideas of being coerced ("trapped") or subject to powerful coercive or invasive influences—such as hypnosis—which weaken or violate the integrity of the will or, in some cases, the body. In the extreme case, the experience of an internal struggle of will is replaced almost entirely by a defensive struggle against external antagonists of the will, with only the sensation of a threatened or weakened will remaining of the original internal experience.

Can projection, understood in this way, be described as a defense "mechanism"? It is not, in my opinion, a satisfactory description. Projection is not a device; it is an outcome of a process, a tendency of the organism under certain conditions of increasing tension—which is to say not so much that projection relieves tension as that it forestalls an intolerable development of tension. The rigid and defensive person experiencing an intensification of internal conflict—and therefore an intensified sense of vulnerability—stiffens further. He stiffens both physically and psychologically; he cannot do otherwise. He stiffens before he becomes more than dimly conscious of that vulnerability. That stiffened defensiveness and the suspicious, ultimately projective, creation of an antagonist are the manifestations of a rigid defensive will mobilized into a state of hyper-rigidity. The defensive engagement with a specific antagonist restores focus and purpose to an individual to whom focus and purpose are essential and forestalls further development of the sensation of internal conflict.

I shall now consider further the nature of certain internal conflicts that are responsible for the intensification of defensiveness.

The Schreber Case and
Freud's Theory of Paranoia

Freud proposed, as is well known, that the exciting cause of
paranoia is an abhorrent unconscious homosexual wish, and
that the paranoid delusion in effect constitutes a denial of that
wish. He developed the theory principally in his famous case
study of the paranoid schizophrenic, Daniel Paul Schreber,[1]
whose primary delusion consisted of the idea that he was being
transformed against his will into a woman, initially by his
psychiatrist, Paul Flechsig, and later by God, for purposes of
sexual abuse. Freud concluded that the figure who became
Schreber's persecutor in the paranoid delusion, Dr. Flechsig,
was the very one to whom Schreber wished unconsciously to
surrender sexually. Freud's case study, first published in 1911,
was based on Schreber's own published *Memoirs*, (1903)[2] a
lengthy, detailed, and extraordinary presentation by Schreber
of his psychotic ideas and experiences.

The main thesis of Freud's paper has become, as Knight has
said,[3] among the most generally accepted and widely
confirmed ideas of psychoanalysis. As far as the case of
Schreber itself is concerned, the evidence in the *Memoirs*
seems irrefutable and must be encompassed by any further
theory of paranoia that can claim interest. Such a theory need
not agree with the central causal significance that Freud assigned to homosexuality in paranoia, but it must account for
the relationship he discovered—and account for it even if that

[1]Sigmund Freud, "Psychoanalytic Notes upon an Autobiographical Account of a
Case of Paranoia," *Collected Papers*, vol. III, (London: Hogarth Press and Institute
of Psychoanalysis, 1949), pp. 387–470.
[2]Daniel P. Schreber, *Memoirs of My Nervous Illness*, translated by Ida MacAlpine
and Richard A. Hunter (London: William Dawson, 1955).
[3]Robert P. Knight, "The Relationship of Latent Homosexuality to the Mechanism
of Paranoid Delusions," *Bulletin of the Menninger Clinic* (1940) 4: 149–59.

relationship does not necessarily hold for every case of a paranoid condition, as I believe it does not, particularly not for women. Indeed, such a theory must account for that relationship even if it turns out, as it certainly has not, that in the Schreber case alone was homosexuality central.

Any new theory of paranoia must attempt also to answer certain questions that were raised by Freud's theory but that could not, as Freud himself realized, be answered by it. I am referring to the general question of the relationship of such abhorrent homosexual wishes to the workings of the paranoid process and to the particular form and nature of paranoid symptoms, attitudes, and thought. I am referring also to such specific questions as those raised clearly by Knight when, speaking of the incompletenesses of Freud's theory, he pointed out, "It does not explain why the paranoiac developed such an intense homosexual wish fantasy, nor why he must deny it so desperately."[4]

Now to turn to the Schreber case itself. I will try to show how his delusion of being forcibly transformed into a female can be understood as a transformation of an inner struggle of will into a defensive struggle of wills with external figures, and also that an understanding of the homosexual conflict in its relationship to the general problem of autonomy is capable of resolving some of the problems raised by Freud's study.

At the age of fifty-one, within weeks after assuming his duties as presiding judge of the Court of Appeals at Dresden, Daniel Paul Schreber, son of a well-known orthopedic physician and author of works on child rearing, suffered a mental breakdown for the second time. The earlier episode (eight years before) had been diagnosed as severe hypochondriasis and had required a hospitalization of six months. This second and far

[4]Ibid., p. 149.

more serious breakdown was preceded by what Schreber came to regard as several significant experiences. During the period following notification of his promotion but before actually assuming his new position, he dreamed on several occasions that his previous mental illness had recurred, and was relieved each time, upon waking, to realize that he had been only dreaming. On another occasion, either in a dream or before completely waking he had the "highly peculiar" thought that "it really must be rather pleasant to be a woman succumbing to intercourse"—an idea that he "would have rejected with indignation" if fully awake.[5] Shortly after assuming his new position as presiding judge, he suffered increasing sleeplessness and agitation. He consulted Dr. Flechsig who had treated him successfully for the previous breakdown, but this time his condition almost immediately worsened. He was admitted to the sanatorium, where he became extremely agitated, hallucinatory, and delusional and made repeated suicide attempts. He believed that he was being tortured at the direction of Dr. Flechsig (although he later came to believe that this was with God's connivance and even at God's instigation), and that Flechsig was attempting to commit "soul murder" on him and transform him into a woman for sexual purposes. In the course of time, the agitated, acute phase of the psychosis subsided, and an exceedingly complicated delusional structure developed. Schreber came to believe that his transformation into a woman was actually taking place; that, though originally against his will, it was decreed by God and accomplished by divine miracles; that it was necessitated by his special relationship to God; and that it was his mission to redeem the world and, having been impregnated by divine rays, to create a new race.

[5] Schreber, *Memoirs* [2], p. 63.

Schreber's originally horrifying idea of transformation into a woman, his "unmanning," actually had a wider significance and was more complicated than a transformation of sex alone. It involved, for example, much more than the threat of emasculation. For the transformation that Schreber struggled against was from the beginning a transformation not merely from man to woman but from a dutiful, upright, "morally unblemished,"[6] dignified, rather ascetic man to a "female harlot."[7] It is a transformation from a person of self-control and will power to a creature dominated by erotic sensuality ("voluptuousness"). His struggle against sexual transformation in the acute phase of the psychosis is, at the same time, a struggle against the undermining of his *manly will* principally by the insinuation into his body of "female nerves."

I was kept in bed and my clothes removed to make me—as I believed —*more amenable* to voluptuous sensations, which could be stimulated in me by the female nerves which had already started to enter my body; medicines were also used; these therefore I refused or spat out again when an attendant poured them forcibly into my mouth. Having, as I thought, definitely come to realize this abominable intention, one may imagine how my whole sense of manliness and manly honor, my entire moral being, rose up against it.[8]

The fact that this was not merely a physical assault or an attempt at emasculation, that it was an assault on Schreber's will with the aim of making him more "amenable," explains that it aroused not merely fear but rather his "manly honor" and "moral being" against it. Indeed, he says that "any manner of death, however frightful, was preferable to so degrading an end."[9]

[6]Ibid., p. 214.
[7]Ibid., p. 77.
[8]Ibid., p. 76. Author's italics.
[9]Ibid.

That Schreber's struggle is one of manly honor and self-control against, specifically, female sensuality and "voluptuousness" is clear throughout the *Memoirs*. He repeatedly identifies *femaleness* with *erotic sensuality*. Thus, he maintains that "nerves of voluptuousness exist over the whole of the female body whereas in the male in the sexual organs and their proximity only . . ."[10] and, "the feeling of sensual pleasure—whatever its physiological basis—occurs in the female to a higher degree than the male, involves the whole body . . . the mammae particularly . . ."[11]

This distinction between the sexes, which also implies a distinction of station, is present even after death among souls: "The male state of Blessedness was superior to the female state; the latter seems to have consisted mainly in an uninterrupted feeling of voluptuousness."[12]

Schreber's struggle against succumbing to voluptuous sensation was, indeed, consciously a struggle of will.

For over a year therefore the female nerves, or nerves of voluptuousness, which had penetrated my body in great masses, could not gain any influence on my behavior or on my way of thinking. I suppressed every feminine impulse by exerting my sense of manly honor and also by the holiness of my religious ideas. . . . On the other hand, my will power could not prevent the occurrence, particularly when lying in bed, of a sensation of voluptuousness.[13]

In fact, the destruction of will and of self-control appears to be the approximate meaning for Schreber of "soul murder," as far as he reveals the meaning at all. Thus, in the measured and

[10]Ibid., p. 204.
[11]Ibid., p. 205.
[12]Ibid., p. 52.
[13]Ibid., p. 120.

rather conciliatory letter to Flechsig with which the *Memoirs* are prefaced, Schreber suggests that

perhaps all the talk of voices about somebody having committed soul murder can be explained by the souls (rays) deeming it impermissible that a person's nervous system should be influenced by another's to the extent of imprisoning his will power, such as occurs during hypnosis; in order to stress forcefully that this was a malpractice it was called "soul murder."[14]

There is a further sense in which the transformation into a woman, as Schreber imagines it, involves a surrender of will. It will be recalled that his psychosis was ushered in with the dreamed or half-awake thought that "it really must be rather pleasant to be a woman succumbing to intercourse."[15] Schreber's fantasy reflects a wish whose direction and object we describe as homosexual. But as a fantasy of a sexual action, it also has a mode suggested in the notion of succumbing. To succumb, to submit, to give in, to surrender—this is the female sexual mode to Schreber, and it was the common understanding of his time and is, to some extent, of ours as well. Thus, the fantasy of being transformed into a female and the idea of female sexuality contain for Schreber both kinds of surrender of will that I have already referred to in connection with sexual masochism: surrender of self-control—that is, surrender to erotic sensuality—on the one hand, and surrender to subjugation, on the other. As I have suggested, to rigid individuals these may have a certain subjective equivalence: both kinds of

[14]Ibid., p. 35.

[15]The operative word is translated by Strachey as "submitting" in Freud's quotation of the sentence ("Psychological Notes upon Paranoia," [1]). MacAlpine's and Hunter's translation (Schreber, *Memoirs* [1])—"succumbing"—has an additional connotation of giving in to the self, while Strachey's indicates only giving in to another. The distinction is not critical here—I have assumed a primary sense of giving in to another; but the apparent ambiguity underscores, if anything, the point that follows.

surrender may be erotic, and certainly both are abhorrent. I shall refer again to this matter shortly.

In time, Schreber "reconciled" himself to his transformation and even embraced it. He was able to do so in a way that did not sacrifice his self-respect and, in fact, so transvalued meanings and circumstances as to change what would have been a humiliating surrender into an accomplishment of will. He came to regard it as his *duty* to cultivate voluptuousness. This "change of will" was not for reasons of "low sensousness" but to serve God. Thus, he realized that for him, "moral limits to voluptuousness no longer exist, indeed, in a certain sense the reverse applies"; and it became his duty to "strive to give divine rays the impression of a woman in the height of sexual delight."[16]

It is not my point to offer an alternative to the homosexual significance of Schreber's idea that he was being transformed into a woman; but I want to show that that idea and his initial abhorrence of that transformation had a further significance. The fantasy of feminization contained not only a sexual direction but, for him, the idea of a total surrender—the whole surrender of manly dignity, self-control, and moral standards to a debased, female, erotic sensuality. This fact—that Schreber's inner conflict over homosexuality is also the struggle of will of a rigid character to maintain mastery of himself, to maintain the whole regime of the will—makes it possible to understand both the special intensity of that struggle and its transformation into a specifically paranoid form. For it is precisely such a struggle of will that can be transformed into a projective struggle of wills with external figures. In such a character, in other words, the experience of temptation to female sexual surrender as a surrender of the will—or, indeed, any sensation

---

[16]Schreber, *Memoirs* [2], p. 208.

of weakness of the will (which rigid men invariably experience as "feminine" weakness or softness)—intensifies the defensive and, ultimately, projective anticipation of humiliation and coercion, particularly at the hands of those figures who are the objects of such temptation.

What of the homosexual impulses themselves? Is the underlying homosexual wish an independent factor whose abhorrence may even have contributed to the development of such rigidity of character, as its intensification now triggers an intensification of rigidity? Or, to the contrary, is the homosexual wish actually a product of, or an aspect of, this form of rigid character? These questions prompt a related one specifically in connection with Schreber's breakdown. If Schreber's paranoia was the immediate consequence of an intensification of homosexual impulses, was this intensification of independent origins, or was it an early manifestation of his breakdown, of the destabilization of his rigid character?

All rigid persons are under the sway of images of superior authority and are to one degree or another ambivalent in their feelings toward figures of authority: exorbitantly respectful, admiring, imitative, on the one hand; resistant, defensive, resentful, on the other. In stable, compulsive people this ambivalence is less intense. It is limited to the extent that a genuine self-respect and sense of personal authority have been achieved. But to the extent that these have not been achieved—I am speaking here of the less stable, more paranoid individual—figures of authority and rank take on greater importance and absorb interest. To him, they become objects of intense respect and admiration, in the way people often respect and admire their rulers, and therefore also of prideful resentment and defensive antagonism. The fact that the paranoid individual tends to rail against certain figures of authority, disparaging them and attempting to diminish their status—the fact, in other words, that this respect is grudging and sour and full of a sense of his own inferior status—cannot disguise, except to himself, that it is respect nonetheless. These superior figures are constantly on his mind. He wants to win their respect, to be recognized, appreciated, and prized by them, to be useful to them, to serve them, to be their protégé. For the paranoid individual, to become an instrument of such authority and will is to experience a sense of strength and authority, as in a lesser way the compulsive person gains a sense of authority from identification with a dogma. Yet the rigid, prideful paranoid person detests such feelings in himself. He regards them, if conscious of them at all, as acknowledgments of his own inferiority, as demeaning and humiliating. Typically, he is only dimly aware of these feelings; they are displaced from consciousness by the defensive feelings, particularly defensive anger, which they generate. Thus, the paranoid person is usually only fleetingly aware of his own sense of inferiority to such figures of authority and of the extent and nature of his own interest in them; but he is extremely, often angrily, sensitive to any indignity, condescension, or rebuff at their hands.

Freud discovered a further, sexual, aspect of this ambivalence, which gives rise to its own defensiveness and projective ideas. Actually, we have already encountered just such a sexual tendency in rigid characters. I am referring to sexual masochism, which depends precisely upon the relationship of inferior to superior and on the special eroticism for the rigid character of female sexual surrender—in other words, to that frame of mind which finds erotic the idea of a subordinate, inferior, humiliating position and of submission to superior power, often an idea of female submission to superior male power. I will not repeat the analysis of this sexual interest beyond saying that, for the person of rigid will and self-control, the image of sexual surrender seems to be especially erotic because it is an image of the surrender of the will, of all restraint and resistance, a giving-in to the other which is, at the same time, a giving-in to the self. And the more rigidly and exaggeratedly "manly" that will, the more likely it is that the image of surrender will be female. Thus, the questions, why should fantasies of female sexual surrender be especially abhorrent to men of this rigid makeup? and, why should such fantasies be especially erotic to them? turn out to have the same answer. The idea of female sexual surrender is for these men an idea of unrestrained and will-less eroticism—an idea, in Schreber's language, of "voluptuousness," of the eroticism of the "female harlot." Thus, the underlying wish to become the instrument of a strong and authoritative figure reaches its culmination in the fantasy of female sexual surrender to such a figure.

Not all concern—among rigid or paranoid men—with weakness, unmanliness, effeminacy, or homosexuality can be regarded, however, as a reflection of conflict about unconscious homosexual wishes. These men, as a rule, abhor not only the idea of female sexual surrender but also the whole —to them "female"—mode of weakness, softness, and giving in. This mode is repugnant to them and disturbing to their pride and self-respect not only because it is a mode of sexual surrender, nor merely because it is (to them) female, but also because it is in itself inimical to a rigid and exaggeratedly masculine will, to "masculine" strength, self-control and dignity, and therefore raises the specter of effeminacy or homosexuality. Specters of will-lessness or weakness of the will in one form or another arise among all rigid characters in conflict. These specters, however—as when a rigidly dutiful and industrious person imagines that if he succumbs to the impulse to put his work aside temporarily, he will "never do anything again"—do not necessarily reflect that conflict accurately but may reflect the distortion and exaggeration of it by inner concern and prejudice. For many men—both paranoid and not paranoid—who are under the sway of rigid and artificial images of manliness, the specter of unmanliness, effeminacy, or homosexuality is raised by whole categories of feeling, interest, or behavior that they abhor as passive, weak, soft—hence, feminine. Thus, they repudiate the emotional, in general, in favor of the rational, the artistic in favor of the practical, and, in sexual relations, not only the feminine or homosexual but also the romantic or even affectionate in favor of business-like, purposeful, no-nonsense sex.

For example, a compulsive but not paranoid man could not bring himself to tell his wife he loved her because that would be "mushy" and sentimental. If he allowed himself to tell her, he "would never get another hard-on in [his] life." In other words, the prospect of a relaxation of "masculine" dignity, restraint, and self-control raised the specter not only of weakness but also of a kind of "unmanning."

To return to Schreber. Freud has little to say about why Schreber should have experienced an intensification of homo-sexual interest at that particular time, beyond the tentative observation that, at the age of fifty-one, Schreber had reached the "male climacteric." The explanation is not persuasive and besides, as William Niederland[17] points out, would hardly apply to Schreber's previous breakdown nine years earlier. On the contrary, it seems that both episodes were related to certain external events of Schreber's career: an unsuccessful candidacy for political office in the first instance and his judicial appoint-

[17]William G. Niederland, *The Schreber Case: Psychoanalytic Profile of a Paranoid Personality* (New York: Quadrangle, 1974).

ment in the second. Schreber himself relates his second breakdown to "the extraordinary burden of work" involved in assuming this new office, unrelieved by the social distraction he was
used to on account of this position also being in a new city. The
first signs of the impending trouble actually occurred, however,
before he assumed these new responsibilities although after he
had been notified of his appointment. It was during this period
that he dreamed that his earlier breakdown had recurred, and
it was then also that he experienced the "peculiar" idea that
"it must be rather pleasant to be a woman succumbing to
intercourse."

Niederland says, "Instead of running *for* office or accepting
an appointment to a high office, he had to run *from* it, driven
by his castration fantasies, which were set in motion the very
moment the dreaded masculine role threatened to become a
reality."[18] This analysis of presumably unconscious conflict
says nothing of the attitudes of consciousness and the kinds of
conscious experience that were involved. It is reasonable to
suppose that this dutiful man experienced his new high position as a presumption from the time of his appointment. We
know, in fact, that at least from the time he assumed office, and
very likely before, he was acutely conscious of being junior in
both age and experience to the other members of the court
over which he was to preside. Of his colleagues, he writes that
"almost all of them were much senior to me (up to twenty
years) and anyway they were much more intimately acquainted
with the procedure of the Court, to which I was a new-
comer."[19]

There is little doubt either that a sense of being in a position
beyond his competency or his proper station expressed itself
from the beginning in a rather defensive concern with the

[18]Ibid., p. 41.
[19]Schreber, *Memoirs* [2], p. 63.

attitudes of his older colleagues and other members of the court toward him, with winning their approbation and forestalling their criticism. This concern, indeed, turns out to be a significant part of what he means by the "extraordinary burden of work" he had to contend with. He says, in explaining the strain of preparing himself for his new office: "I was driven . . . to achieve first of all the necessary respect among my colleagues and others concerned with the Court (barristers, and so on) by unquestionable efficiency."[20]

To experience one's action or situation as presumptuous[21] —and this was a question not of a momentary act but of a permanent arrangement—is to shrink back, to become acutely and anxiously conscious of oneself, to be reminded, or to be prompted to remind oneself, of one's inadequacies and one's proper, and lesser, place. And this reaction is especially true of a dutiful and conscientious man. For such a person, in other words, such a situation and experience may shake the normal sense of competence, confidence of purpose, and authority. It may be assumed also that the anxiety prompted in Schreber by his new situation was further intensified by the particular anxiety about himself (which, by the time he consulted Flechsig again, had reached the point of panic) reflected in his dreams about the recurrence of his previous "nervous illness."

Let me say, then, that this rigid man who seems hardly to have thought himself capable of weakness of will or uncertainty of purpose was in fact already in a weakened, anxious, some-

---

[20]Ibid.

[21]Another, striking evidence that Schreber experienced his new status and position as presumptuous is contained in one of his later delusional ideas in which the "rays of God" mockingly say to him, "so *this* sets up to have been a Senätsprasident, this person who lets himself be fucked!" (quoted in Freud, Psychoanalytic Notes upon Paranoia [1], pp. 399–400). The MacAlpine and Hunter translation (Schreber, *Memoirs* [2]) of this passage is quite different, however; it reverses the emphasis of the clauses and does not convey the sense of presumption to the same degree: "Fancy a person who was a Senätsprasident allowing himself to be fucked."

what defensive condition before he took office, although, if I judge his character correctly, at the time he hardly admitted it to himself. In other words, the sense of masculine dignity, will, and self-control which he later imagined to have been undermined by supernatural forces was actually already undermined to some extent in ways he could not recognize. But weakness and uncertainty of will and purpose have not only their anxieties for a rigid person but also their needs and temptations. It would not be remarkable if at this time Schreber experienced an intensified need, an anxious wish—which normally dignity would have forbidden—for some external form, or some external figure, of authority, strength, and order (Flechsig?). Nor would it be remarkable or inconsistent with Schreber's rigid, ascetic character if he had experienced, precisely when the regime of masculine will was shaken, the temptations of "voluptuous" erotic fantasies—for him, fantasies of female sexual surrender. We know with certainty only of his isolated thought of "succumbing to intercourse" (and we know of it precisely because he did not understand its significance). Indeed, he attributes his tolerance of that fantasy at the time to a (momentary) condition of weakness, the fact that he was not fully awake, and adds, with a characteristic assertion of will, "This idea was so foreign to my whole nature that I may say I would have rejected it with indignation if fully awake."[22] Not for a moment could he entertain the notion that it was in fact not foreign to his nature. Consequently his conscious sense of the wishes contained in this dream or fantasy, and of any other of the needs or sensations of his disturbed state, was probably limited largely to the increasingly anxious sense that something "peculiar," ominous, and finally abhorrent was happening to him.

[22]Schreber, *Memoirs* [2], p. 63.

Schreber did of course return to Dr. Flechsig and submit once again to his authority and care. We cannot know the relation, if any, between the fantasy of female sexual surrender and Schreber's wish to place himself again under Flechsig's care. It is possible that the wish to return to Flechsig gave rise to the fantasy of sexual surrender, but it is equally possible that the two wishes to "give in," if one may put it so, were originally independent of each other, though parallel. At any rate, one may surmise that the decision to return to Dr. Flechsig was also an ambivalent one.

From certain remarks in the *Memoirs,* one can judge that Schreber's attitude toward Professor Flechsig had been ambivalent since Flechsig's successful treatment of his first breakdown. These remarks, even if one allows for the fact that they reflect a later perspective, make it clear enough that Schreber's gratitude to Flechsig was dutiful and grudging, and that his respect and admiration was mingled with a prideful resentment at his having been obliged, even then, to submit to certain (medical) indignities. He says, referring to that earlier treatment:

I had on the whole only favorable impressions of Professor Flechsig's methods of treatment. Some mistakes may have been made . . . white lies . . . were hardly ever appropriate in my case, for . . . he was dealing with a human being of high intellect. . . . I believe I could have been more rapidly cured . . . if I had been allowed to operate the scale . . . a few times myself. . . . All the same these are only minor points . . . perhaps it is unreasonable to expect . . . [etc.].[23]

[23]Ibid., p. 62.

When he returned to Flechsig in an extremely disturbed state on the second occasion, however, his immediate relief was very great. Flechsig assured him of the possibilities of treatment, and Schreber speaks of being deeply affected by Flechsig's "remarkable eloquence." Indeed it does not seem too much to say that Schreber immediately and gratefully—if only briefly—surrendered to the spell of this impressive figure. Almost at once, however, there is a striking suggestion of resistance to following the very prescription that Flechsig had just given him. Flechsig had given him hope of a cure through "one prolific sleep, which was to start, if possible, at three o'clock in the afternoon." Although he immediately obtained the necessary sleeping drug, Schreber says, "Naturally [!] I did not get to bed (in my mother's house) as early as 3 o'clock, but (possibly according to some secret instruction which my wife had received) it was delayed until the 9th hour."[24] At any rate, the attempt at sleep was not successful; that night he attempted suicide, and the next morning he entered the asylum. In the following days he was manifestly psychotic and delusional; initially, his ideas were evidently dominated by hypochondriacal delusions (such as softening of the brain) followed shortly by ideas of persecution.

Schreber's defensive and projective struggle against Flechsig's efforts to degrade and "unman" him had a precursor in the earlier ambivalent and defensive relationship to Flechsig's authority. Those struggles may even be regarded as an intensification and an extension of that ambivalence. One may imagine Schreber always to have been sensitive about and defensive of his dignity before those he actually regarded as his superiors, divided between deference to their authority and prideful defense of his own. If my picture is correct, the destabilization of his disciplined, probably compulsive, adjustment—his diminished sense of authority and weakened will—intensified both aspects of this ambivalence: on the one hand, it raised the temptation, though he could not recognize it, of total abandonment of manly discipline and honor and the will-less, voluptuous surrender to the admired Flechsig; on the other hand, the abhorrent and peculiar sensations of these wishes, the sensation of something "foreign to his nature" and subversive of his will intensified his defensiveness and turned his suspicions toward Flechsig—in a sense correctly—as its cause.

The Schreber case has gained additional interest in recent years owing to the research of William Niederland into the writings of Schreber's father.[25] This new information offers an extraordinary opportunity to understand certain aspects of the development of Schreber's character.

The elder Schreber, apparently a well-known authority on child rearing as well as a physician, advocated and presumably subjected his own children to an extraordinary regimen of psychological and physical coercion and restraint in accordance with his theories of achieving physical and mental health, upright posture, and upright character.

In order to achieve these results, for example, Dr. Schreber devised various orthopedic appliances—belts, straps, and braces of various sorts—to be used during sleep as well as waking hours; their purpose was to maintain correctness of posture and to prevent the child from falling into an undesirable position. Such appliances were only a part of a total program. Niederland says:

[25]Niederland, *Schreber Case* [17].

Besides elaborate prescriptions for daily gymnastics and methodical calisthenics . . . we find [in one of the father's books] . . . detailed rules for every action during almost every hour in the regular routine of the child's life. There are minute and inflexible instructions for the child's total behavior, including its orderliness and cleanliness which "must be made the supreme law." Rules are specified for ritualistic pre-breakfast or pre-lunch walking exercises with "no deviation allowed from the once established procedure."[26]

The more or less explicit aim of this regimen was to break the child's will. Thus Dr. Schreber says that

"crying and whimpering without reason express nothing but a whim, a mood, and the first emergence of stubbornness; they must be dealt with positively . . . and then one is master of the child forever."[27]

Niederland says that young Schreber "appears to have been forced into complete submission and passive surrender by a father whose sadism may have been but thinly disguised under a veneer of medical, reformatory, religious and philanthropic ideas."[28] Actually, the proposition that Schreber was forced into "complete submission and passive surrender" is open to argument. The fact is that it was neither the aim of Dr. Schreber's regimen simply to produce a passive, submissive, "weak" individual, nor its result, at least in the case of his son. Dr. Schreber's aim in breaking the child's own will was, on the contrary, to re-form it, to build a "strong" character, an individual capable of self-control and self-discipline.

This aim is strikingly evident, for example, in the training in "renouncing" that Dr. Schreber recommended for the child's first year: the nurse is to eat or drink while the child sits on her lap, but the child is not permitted a morsel.

[26]Ibid.
[27]Ibid., p. 71.
[28]Ibid., p. 70.

Such aims and attitudes—the aims and attitudes of the fanatical disciplinarian and moralist—are, moreover, not only a veneer or a disguise for sadism; sadism is also an intrinsic part of them. Such fanatical moralism always contains, and often not so unconsciously, a contempt for and a hatred of weakness and softness and a sadistic urge to punish them. In other words, the idea of such punishing discipline for the sake of character building is a product of much the same attitudes and frame of mind that give rise to the driven urge to sadistic punishment and to "discipline" for its own sake. The moralism and the sadism are, so to speak, continuous with one another and regularly exist together, the one to some extent obscuring the other.

At any rate, Dr. Schreber's aims were more complicated, and the methods required to implement them more systematic, than would be required, for example, to reduce a child to mere submission to the whim or the arbitrary force of an adult. Dr. Schreber aimed, by a regimen of highly systematic coercion, not merely to force submission to a *person* but to an inner program—to rules, principles, and so on, and to instill respect for *their* authority as well as for their author. He aimed that the child should embrace these rules as his own, that they would supersede the child's own "ignoble" inclinations and wishes in directing behavior. To put the matter another way, the aim of this coercive regimen was to destroy one kind of autonomy and install another in its place and to force acceptance not only of the adult's command but also of the adult's standards and precepts—to force acceptance of them as his own and identification with their point of view. The result was to be not submissiveness but a new kind of will founded in authoritarian strictness and coercive self-control. In this sense Dr. Schreber's aims and methods were not remarkably different from the training aims and methods of the Marine Corps. In both cases the initial submission to coercive discipline is followed by identification with that discipline; thus what might have been, so to speak, an experience of surrender is transformed into one of self-mastery and strength, even manly strength. In such coercive circumstances, in which autonomy is subdued and feelings of powerlessness and perhaps shame threaten to become intense, this kind of identification may be the only avenue to self-respect. In any case, such an identification, far from being mere passive surrender, is actually an alternative to passive surrender; and, in fact, one of its consequences is an abhorrence of weakness and surrender.

It is true that an identification of this kind cannot be complete or completely stable; that it is necessarily rigid; that—along with a sense of strength and self-mastery—it contains, as in a rigid sense of duty, a subjective aspect of obedience and submission. And it is true, as Schreber's case illustrates, that if the rigid identification is shaken, the wish for some figure of authority and the temptation, perhaps including the sexual temptation, to abandon one's will to his, may be intensified. But just because such a surrender remains abhorrent, it gives rise not to mere submissiveness but to defensive and projective struggles.

To conclude: Neither the existence of unconscious homosexuality nor the revulsion against it is capable of explaining the nature of paranoid pathology; something of the opposite is true. The nature of paranoid rigidity and of the paranoid problem of autonomy is capable of explaining both a special impulse toward and a special abhorrence for "female" sexual surrender —in men, a homosexual impulse. If my reasoning has been correct, however, neither the impulse nor the abhorrence of it necessarily occupies the essential role in the development of paranoia, even in men, which Freud assigned to them. It appears that the intensification of the homosexual wish is itself a special manifestation of the destabilization of a certain kind of male rigidity, which then exacerbates and often becomes the focus of defensive and projective processes. It is, therefore, a regular feature of male paranoia. It is possible also that a special degree of unconscious homosexual interest may be an aspect of the instability of rigid character which predisposes to paranoia in men. But no apparent reason in the logic of paranoia requires that it invariably be so. We know, in fact, that many kinds of internal and external circumstance, apart from the intensification of homosexual impulses, are capable of intensifying, at least temporarily, the sense of vulnerability, defensiveness, and projective distortion in already defensive, rigid characters.

Indeed, if I am right, homosexuality does not occupy the same place in paranoia in women as in men; and the relationship as applied to women has not, in fact, had the same general acceptance. Perhaps, in female paranoid conditions with apparent homosexual tendencies, it is not so much the homosexual—that is, the masculine—inclination that is repudiated but again the impulse to a "female" surrender of will which is abhorrent to a rigid, prideful "masculine" point of view. In some paranoid women, it seems possible that certain heterosexual experiences or fantasies of sexual surrender may have played a role in the intensification of shame and defensiveness and in the development of projective ideas comparable with homosexual wishes in men. In any event, the objective category of a sexual wish, homosexual/heterosexual, masculine/feminine does not unambiguously or exhaustively define its subjective experience and significance: For example, as the case of Schreber itself shows, a female sexual wish may be abhorrent when one experiences it as surrender, but acceptable when one see it as a moral duty.

The Problem of
Paranoid Schizophrenia

Extreme paranoid conditions regularly take on features of schizophrenia, and any theory of paranoia must explain this relationship. If paranoia is actually a pathology of autonomy, a condition of extreme rigidity, then it is necessary to understand why such a condition, upon reaching a certain degree of severity, increasingly takes on schizophrenic features.

As I have said, any rigidity of self-direction necessarily involves restriction and curtailment of one's interest in the world, distortion of one's experience of it, and, in the final analysis, a loss of an objective relationship to it. The more severe the rigidity, the greater this loss. I have already referred to instances of such loss in the case of obsessional and compulsive people. The fact that, to one extent or another, the aims and purposes of these individuals are determined by pre-established rules rather than by the possibilities of their objective circumstances, means that they are frequently in consultation with themselves when others are interested in the world. The compulsive person is concerned with what he *should* order when other people are interested in the menu. His interest in the world is restricted to technical data relevant to authoritative rules—Is the job done according to the book? Is the woman an "appropriate" companion?—with a corresponding loss of interest in the thing itself—the actual problem, the actual woman. Similarly, his reliance on the authority of dogma, the "party line," restricts his interest, diminishes his awareness of the shadings of things, and replaces the normal sense of truth and conviction with reliance on authoritative inference: it "must" be so, or it "cannot" be so. Even the obsessional person's worrying, driven by the conscientious requirement to pay special respect and special attention to the possibility of misfortune, means that he loses a sense of the actual proportions of things, of their relative significance and probability.

In all these instances, the intrusion of authority in the form of a priori rules and requirements for the direction of interest has narrowed and prejudiced experience of the world and has done so not merely in particular matters but in its general form. And this loss of full experience of the world's objective quality is directly traceable to the distortion of the processes of self-direction in rigid character.

In paranoid conditions, rigidity is much more severe, and so is the loss of objectification. The defensive mobilization of will against external threat introduces the most rigid and restrictive kind of bias into the paranoid individual's attitude toward the world. To put the matter simply, openmindedness is a luxury that those who feel vulnerable cannot afford. The necessity to penetrate the deception, to identify the threat, to overlook no ominous significance; the further necessity to avoid distraction from these efforts or any relaxation of them, to avoid the possibility of being deceived, of being taken by surprise—these requirements severely restrict and bias the nature of experience. The person who feels vulnerable in this way must respect anything that suggests the possibility of personal threat, however remote, and must distrust anything that appears to be innocuous. He cannot be certain about what appears to be innocuous and, therefore, cannot with safety regard it as actually being so, as containing no hidden threat, as being other than deception. Therefore, he must scrutinize further everything that appears to be innocuous, harmless, or impersonal for the threat it may yet contain, or brush it aside as mere appearance.

In the final analysis, such an individual can be satisfied that he is not being deceived only when he has identified a threat.

Nothing else can quiet his sense of vulnerability, guarantee against his being fooled or being surprised, against gullibility, complacency, sentimentality. It is inevitable, in other words, that the individual with such a bias will finally discover a threat. It is inevitable that he will find at least an element of ambiguity in what appears to be harmless and at least an element of threat in what seems ambiguous.

The product of this point of view is not merely particular projective ideas but a general distortion of experience. The rigidity, the disciplined bias and the restriction of its interest, and ultimately the seizing of clues and dismissal of their context, constitute a general loss of objectivity and of a sense of proportion far more severe, for example, than the case of obsessional worry. The English critic, Max Beerbohm,[29] described the intelligence of a certain writer as the kind that sees through a brick wall, and added that, of course, such a person cannot see the wall itself. Out of a rigid defensive bias, a world can be constructed of signs and clues, hidden relations and hidden significances—a world of self-reference and threat.

Paranoid people, in other words, are unusually acute and sensitive in their observations, as they have special reason to be and as intensely biased people always are, but it is a highly selective sensitivity. This rigid and unrecognized selectiveness imposes an interpretive structure on the world, a structure of personal significance, which makes use of certain objective data but does not reflect an objective relationship with the world. It is the respectful consciousness of the context of things that have personal subjective significance, consciousness of their size and proportions and, above all, of their significance from other angles and in other relationships, that distinguishes an attitude of objectivity from, in Piaget's sense, an egocentric or

[29]S. N. Behrman, *Portrait of Max* (New York: Random House, 1960).

a subjective attitude. Such an objective attitude contains a sense of the separateness of the world and, at the same time, of the separateness of the self, of the existence of one's personal point of view, and of the distinction between the personally significant and the objective. In short, such an attitude guarantees the polarity between the self and the external world. Lacking it, one can find evidence to substantiate any bias; unknowingly, an objective relationship with the world is replaced by egocentricity and subjectivity. Thus, the rigid bias of defensiveness leads to the repeated "discovery" of the unrecognized products of its own concerns and preoccupations.

With increased defensive tension and, consequently, greater rigidity of bias, the discovery of the external threat becomes both more certain and more immediate. The paranoid person's thought and judgment become so narrowly restricted by the requirements of guardedness and the necessity to anticipate threat, and by dread of surprise and deception, as to forbid increasingly any point of view except that of defensive bias. His detachment and critical judgment are lost. There is no genuine thinking-about, considering, objective reality. His interest is triggered by and limited to clues that satisfy his expectancies; there is nothing further to consider. There remains only the explication, the unfolding, of unrecognized prejudices.

For example, to Schreber, the idea that Flechsig had "secret designs" against him "seemed confirmed" by the fact that, during a visit, Flechsig "could no longer . . . look me straight in the eye."[30]

The very rigidity of suspicious thinking, its prejudice and imperviousness to influence, may endow it, just as it does dog-

[30]Schreber, *Memoirs* [2], p. 68.

matism, with a semblance of critical detachment that it does not actually possess. Thus, what may be merely a rigid prejudice that "sees through" all that does not suit it and reacts extravagantly to what does, outwardly resembles a critical and penetrating judgment. Indeed (again, to a lesser degree, as in the case of dogmatism), the rigidly suspicious attitude may contain a certain subjective illusion of mastery, an exaggerated, sometimes even grandiose, sense of encompassing, penetrating comprehension. This is a pseudo mastery; its "comprehension" is contained in the unrecognized tendency of the thought process itself and needs only to be precipitated by suitable bits or pieces of reality.

The more severe the rigidity, the more direct and immediate the response of suspicious bias and anticipation. In the extreme case, even the semblance—or primitive kind—of critical judgment disappears. It is no longer necessary even to "see through" what does not suit the bias; the element that does suit it appears like a signal—immediately, compellingly, and everywhere. The polarity between the self and the external world is lost.

For example, an acutely paranoid individual says that significant personal messages now "jump out" at him from billboards and the radio.

Such impairment of detachment from or objectification of the world is a picture of schizophrenia. An impairment of the quality of thought must always accompany such a severe impairment of objectification. The flexible, consciously intentional, direction of thought and attention requires a vantage point of detachment from which the thinker can regard the object of his interest. When such a vantage point is destroyed by rigidly suspicious bias, thought becomes merely reactive, and in a sense, helpless; stereotyped ideas are triggered—they "jump out"—and dominated by whatever in external reality or in one's thoughts themselves is immediately and associatively significant to that bias. Such an impairment of objectification and of the capacity for flexible and detached direction of thought and attention is the most central of the formal characteristics of schizophrenia. It is the condition described by Goldstein,[31] for example, as a loss of the abstract attitude in schizophrenia; by Blatt and Wild[32] as the loss of boundaries; or by Werner[33] as the "syncretic" thought characteristic of schizophrenia. This essential condition of thought accounts for the variously described classical symptoms of schizophrenia, such as confusion, impairment of concentration, "looseness," or "tangentiality" of thought. These symptoms, in other words, reflect the uncontrolled intrusion into, or contamination of, more detached, intentional, and orderly thought and language by immediate personal and subjective association, although in paranoid schizophrenia, short of the extreme case, the rigidity of thought and preoccupation seems to preserve a degree of primitive directedness and orderliness of thinking against more chaotic intrusion.

It is well known that the condition of schizophrenia harks back to the early lack of polarity between subject and object.

[31]Kurt Goldstein, "Methodological Approach to Schizophrenic Thought Disorder," in J. S. Kasanin, ed., *Language and Thought in Schizophrenia* (New York: W. W. Norton, 1964), pp. 17–39.

[32]Sidney J. Blatt and Cynthia M. Wild, *Schizophrenia, A Developmental Analysis* (New York: Academic Press, 1976) consider the loss of boundaries central in schizophrenia in general, but note significant differences between paranoid schizophrenia and other forms of schizophrenia in this respect. They suggest that the "exaggerated" object articulation of paranoid schizophrenia may be a compensatory attempt to prevent dissolution of boundaries. This exaggerated articulation, however, is actually a rigid, suspicious, stereotyped recognition of object-signals, not a detached, objective articulation, which, like the pseudo comprehension it is part of, disguises an actual loss of boundaries.

[33]Heinz Werner, *Comparative Psychology of Mental Development* (Chicago: Follett, 1948), pp. 331–36.

I have suggested that the development of autonomy or self-direction is tied to the process of objectification—that in fact the development of autonomy and the development of objectification may be aspects of the same process. The fact that the severe impairment of autonomy in paranoia has the direct result of a corresponding impairment of objectification seems to confirm that view.

INDEX

Abstract thought: and abstract attitude, 37–38; in adolescence, 64–68; and objectification, 38, 39, 54; volitional action and, 36–39; impairment of in schizophrenia, 171–72

Acting out, 8

Action, in psychoanalysis, 4, 11–12. *See also* Volitional action

Adolescence: autonomy in, 64–68; psychopathology of, 67–68

Aggression, 103–4; sexual, 123–33. *See also* Masochism; Sadism

Anal character, 102–3

Anatomy of Human Destructiveness, The (Fromm), 103n, 105n, 106n

Anxiety, castration, 123, 157

Authoritarianism, 103, 107n, 108

Authority figures: adolescents and, 66; first relations with, and autonomy, 46–51; identification with, 165; rigid characters and, 73–77, 153–54; self-respect and inferiority feelings and, 55–64

Autonomy: abstract thought and, 36–39; in adolescence, 64–68; authority relationships in childhood and, 46–51,

55–68; early intentionality and, 32–46; Erikson's view of, 35; identification and, 56, 58; masochism and, 101–2, 109–19, 119n (*see also* Masochism); motivation and, 12–19; neurosis and, 5, 23–30; neurotic styles and, 3–4; objectiveness and, 32, 39–46, 51–55, 173; psychotherapy and, 29; in rigid characters, 3–6, 30–31, 69–77; sadism and, 101–9 (*see also* Sadism); in schizophrenia, 28n; and struggles of will, 134–35; subjective experience of, 23–29, 29n, 30n. *See also* Volitional action

Bak, Robert, 120, 120n

Beach, Frank A., 125, 125n

Beauvoir, Simone de, 126n, 127

Beerbohm, Max, 169

Behrman, S. N., 169n

Blatt, Sidney J., 172, 172n

Bogdan, Robert, 62n

Boot camp, 107, 164

Bowel control, 35, 102. *See also* Toilet training